The Dennis Wheatley Library of the Occult
Volume 26

In 1763 a shocked public learned that its
Prime Minister, Chancellor of the Exchequer
and other Cabinet Ministers had for years
been masquerading in the semi-ruined Abbey
of Medmenham on the banks of the Thames.
Not only had they dressed up as 'monks'
and indulged in mysterious rites, but they
had admitted to their strange society
masked and hooded women, whom they
called 'nuns'. When the secret of
Medmenham became known, this rakes'
club transferred its headquarters to caves
cut deep into the heart of West Wycombe
Hill. Posterity has come to know the
originally styled 'Knights of Saint Francis of
Wycombe' as the 'Hell-Fire Club'.

The Dennis Wheatley Library of the Occult

The Hell-Fire Club

The Story of the Amorous Knights of Wycombe

DONALD McCORMICK

SPHERE BOOKS LIMITED
30/32 Gray's Inn Road, London WC1X 8JL

First published in Great Britain
by Jarrolds Publishers (London) Ltd 1958
Copyright © Donald McCormick 1958
Published by Sphere Books 1975
Introduction copyright © Dennis Wheatley 1975

TRADE MARK

Set in Monotype Baskerville

Printed in Great Britain by
C. Nicholls & Company Ltd
The Philips Park Press, Manchester

ISBN 0 7221 5909 9

CONTENTS

INTRODUCTION

No library of the occult would be complete without a volume about the immoral Order of Saint Francis which held its unholy rites first in the ruined Abbey on Medmenham Island, in the Thames, and later in a series of man-made caves under West Wycombe Hill, during the middle of the eighteenth century.

I have chosen this book by Donald McCormick because it was first published in 1958; so the research is more up to date than any of the many other accounts of the doings of those lecherous 'monks' and 'nuns'.

But it must be stated here that in my view the author has done his utmost to whitewash the Order, as he asserts that there is no foundation for the general belief during the past that the rites performed were worship of the Devil. So, if the reader wants descriptions of Black Masses, he must turn to Huysman's *Down There*, Francis Mossiker's *The Affair of the Poisons*, volumes 23 and 28 in this library, or to some of my own books.

Personally, I do not agree with the author. If he is right why, before the Order was established, was its founder, Sir Francis Dashwood, so anxious to obtain that extremely rare book on Satanism which was brought to him in secret one night in 1746 at the Sign of the George and Vulture in Cornhill? The *inner circle* of the Order consisted of thirteen men. Why that particular number unless they formed a Satanic coven? Again there are many accounts of the notorious John Wilkes, a prominent member, having smuggled a baboon, wearing a mask with horns, into a chest under the altar in the chapel of the Abbey, then having released the animal in the middle of a service; upon which the 'monks' panicked and fled in terror. Why should the effect upon them have been so shattering if it was not that they believed they really had raised the Devil?

No, I regard Mr. McCormick's whitewash as very thin, and there is little doubt that Satanic rites were regularly performed at Medmenham Abbey. But the author does produce ample evidence that, with the exception of Lord Sandwich, most of the 'monks' were by no means wicked men; particularly Dashwood himself.

He was the most generous of men and liked by all classes. It is, too, interesting to learn that it was he who inspired and collaborated with the famous American, Benjamin Franklin – another of the 'monks' – in producing a revised and greatly shortened Book of Common Prayer for the Church of England; his reason being not to denigrate the service but 'to prevent the old and faithful from freezing to death through long ceremonies in cold churches, to make the services so short as to attract the young and lively, and to relieve the well-disposed from the infliction of interminable prayers'.

The Hell-Fire Club at Medmenham had many similarly called predecessors and other successors well into the following century. The popular interest shown for over 200 years in this particular one is due to the distinction of the membership. It's founder, Sir Francis Dashwood, was for a year a very incompetent Chancellor of the Exchequer and later, after elevation to the peerage as Lord le Despencer, an exceptionally able Post-Master General. The Prime Minister, the Earl of Bute, was a member in its early days. So were Sandwich, the First Lord of the Admiralty, and Potter, the Paymaster General. Poetry, drama, painting, literature and wit were represented by leading lights of their era: Paul Whitehead, Charles Churchill, Robert Lloyd, George Selwyn and William Hogarth. Among those who are said to have participated from time to time are Frederick, Prince of Wales, the Duke of Kingston, the Marquis of Granby, the Earls of Oxford, March, Westmoreland and many other members of the aristocracy; their common bond, of course, being lecherous revelry with the 'nuns' they brought down from London.

As the book gives so much information about many prominent people of that period, it is certain that lovers of history will enjoy it. And I fully endorse the comparison made by the author near the end of the book between the abilities of the average Member of Parliament in that, in many ways corrupt, era with those of the M.P.s of our own day.

The Dilettante Club, which Dashwood helped to found when only twenty-four years old, still exists with a very limited membership. It owns the fine paintings of the most distinguished 'monks' of Medmenham and, having no premises of its own, has loaned these to the St. James Club, of which I happen to be a member. So when I lunch or dine there I can enjoy being looked down on by the portraits of those gay rakes who disported themselves at the most notorious of all Hell-Fire Clubs.

Dennis Wheatley

AUTHOR'S FORENOTE

When an author deliberately sets out to prove that the title he has given his book is erroneous, he owes his readers at least an explanation for such tergiversation.

The sub-title—*The Story of the Amorous Knights of Wycombe*—is much more accurate. It was in this fashion that contemporaries referred to them, and both at Medmenham Abbey and in West Wycombe Caves there was much more of the scent of perfumed paramours than the smell of brimstone.

But pedantry can be more of a sin than borrowing apt inexactitudes. This strange society of Georgian rakes is still most popularly known as the Hell-Fire Club, and, despite the stigma it gives to its members, this title is at least more indicative of their environment than is the original name of the Knights of 'Saint' Francis of Wycombe.

CHAPTER 1

'IF two Englishmen were to be cast aside on an uninhabited island,' wrote the brothers Goncourt, 'their first consideration would be the formation of a club.'

Since this observation was made in the nineteenth century it has been borrowed, cribbed and improved upon by so many tedious after-dinner speakers that today it is little more than an outdated cliché. Nonetheless, it is a cliché which is an unconscionable time in burying itself. The English still like to think of themselves as a race of clubmen whether on the elevated level of White's or Boodle's, or on the homelier and more bucolic plane of the working man's institute, or an Oddfellows' lodge. The myth that England was ruled by 'clubmen' lived throughout the nineteenth century; it flared into reality at the celebrated Carlton Club meeting in 1922, when the Coalition Government was brought down. It has even been suggested by an august, if not Augustan Sunday newspaper that Mr. Macmillan has shown his 'greatness' as a Premier by 'occasionally walking from No. 10, Downing Street, to meet old friends at the club'.

But in the eighteenth century such polite condescensions to a juvenile conception of democracy were happily unnecessary. It was not the Cabinet Minister who deigned still to find time to visit his club, but the rakish clubman who graciously quaffed his tankard and condescended to give a portion of his time to the affairs of State.

This was truly the golden age of the English club. 'These were not the "co-operative palaces of luxury", which exist now in Pall Mall or St. James's Street,' wrote R. B. Mowat. 'They were simply groups of mutually congenial men who agree to meet once a week or once a fortnight in a certain coffee-house or tavern. They met in order to enjoy the society and conversation of one another. . . . There were thousands of such clubs all over the country.'

There was no snobbish nonsense about membership; the clubs of the eighteenth century were an aristocracy of the spirit, not of blood. A good clubman needed to have no inhibitions, none of that narrow orthodoxy which a century later was to become the death rattle of the aristocracy, blending it into an unholy alliance of middle-class snobbism and a decadent and self-deprecatory élite. The eighteenth century had no time for that modern phenomenon, the well-bred bore. A capacity for being elegantly outrageous was of more importance than a talent for polite insincerities.

Club life had been known spasmodically in England since the Middle Ages. The earliest known club in London was Le Court de Bone Compagnie, which existed in the reign of Henry IV. It was described in detail by the medieval poet, Occleve, and seems to have possessed a spirit of Chaucerian camaraderie. Sir Walter Raleigh is reputed to have founded the Friday Street Club which met at the Mermaid Tavern in Cheapside, while Ben Jonson was a member of the Apollo, whose meetings were at the Devil Tavern, close by Temple Bar. But club life in its modern form – in something more carefully organized than spontaneous tavern gatherings – only began to flourish with the coming of the chocolate and coffee-houses of the seventeenth century. The traditions of Liberal journalism may have arisen from the cocoa trade, but the seventeenth-century cup of chocolate was the beverage on which radical pamphleteering was most truly founded. Pepys, that inveterate preserve of private thoughts, was a member of the Coffee Club and White's (founded in 1693) was really evolved from the Chocolate House Club.

As the coffee and chocolate-houses were used as a serious source of news gathering and for exchanging opinions, it is understandable that the first clubs which sprang up at this time were mainly of a literary character. For, perhaps, the only period in English history the political and social scene was dominated by men of literature. Never before or since have literary men been held in such great respect in a country supposed to be influenced mainly by Philistines.

12

But in the eighteenth century London society accepted, almost without question what amounted to a dictatorship by men of letters. Swift formed the literary coterie known as the Scriblerus, which provoked Pope – because of feeble health a *salon* visitor rather than a clubman – to write his satires on dullness, *The Works of Dr. Scriblerus*. And it is interesting to note that, anticipating Nelson, this club later changed its name to The Band of Brothers. Later the supreme literary arbiter of the day arose in the argumentative but entirely lovable person of Dr. Samuel Johnson, who described the faithful Boswell as 'a very clubbable man'. In fact, it is said that the word 'clubbable' is Johnsonian in origin. Certainly he was club-minded, founding one club in Ivy Street, Paternoster Row, and another at the Essex Head Tavern in Essex Street. Most famous of all these literary organizations, which fulfilled a valuable role in moulding opinion and stimulating the cut and thrust of civilized argument, was the Literary Club, sponsored by Sir Joshua Reynolds, and including Dr. Johnson, Edmund Burke and Dr. Goldsmith among its members.

Not only writers started these literary clubs. One of the best known, the Kit Cat, was founded by Christopher Cat, a cook who was better known for his mutton pies than his literary aspirations. The writers and artists did not have it all their own way for long. Politicians quickly realized the advantages of organizing themselves into similar groups. By the end of the seventeenth century the Sealed Knot, a royalist institution, had aroused considerable controversy, and in 1710 '150 staunch Tories' met at the Bell in Westminster to launch the October Club. Lord Bolingbroke's Saturday Club, the Green Ribbon and the Hanover were other politically inspired bodies, and as the eighteenth century progressed so the nomenclature of clubs became more eccentric. The Calves' Head, started shortly after the execution of Charles I, for the purpose of ceremoniously deriding his memory, lasted until 1734, when it was suppressed after a riot. The dishes served at its annual dinners included a cod's head, symbolizing 'Charles Stuart', a boar's head, said to denote the King's tyranny over his subjects, while the calves' heads depicted the adherents and descendants of the Stuarts.

New clubs sprang up to vie with one another in the oddness of their titles. There was the Golden Fleece in which every member had to assume a characteristic pseudonym, such as Sir Boozy Prate-All, Sir Whore-Hunter and Sir Ollie-Mollie. The last-named eventually broke away from his hearty, wenching, brandy-swilling companions with their robust and Rabelaisian brand of humour to form, by way of contrast, the first of the Mollies' Clubs, which, for a few years, became à la mode for young men. At these gatherings male members dressed up as women, sipping gin and simpering in satins as, giggling behind fans, they cooed to one another:

> 'Tell me, gentle hobdehoy,
> Art thou girl, or art thou boy?'

But this preview of the Green Carnation era of the eighteen-nineties did not predominate in the eighteenth century. The 'Mollies' were merely a reaction from the empty-headed and exaggerated masculinity of the Roaring Boys. They were quickly ridiculed out of existence, for even in the most sophisticated circles it was held that there was an infinite variety of permutations on normal sexual relations without borrowing from Plato and Hadrian.

The quest for perversity was in the realm of ideas rather than of passion. It was exemplified in the Ugly Club, whose members had to pass a test for possessing extreme viciousness of countenance and unpleasing features before election was sanctioned. Those who thirsted for the latest news at the earliest possible moment joined the Wet Paper, which met at the Chapter Coffee House in Paternoster Row, a condition of membership being that they had to read newspapers fresh from the press and before the ink had dried on them. It is noteworthy and perhaps socially significant that the clubs with the eccentric names survived longest, while those which laid claims to omniscience, immortality and pompous grandeur came to a speedy end. Humbug was regarded as the supreme vice of the century, and the Everlasting, which started with the idea that it should go on for ever, soon dissolved, while the Ace of Clubs, aimed at becoming the most exclusive in London, closed down in under a year.

On the other hand the Lying Club, in which downright tergiversation was the essential qualification for membership, flourished exceedingly, most of its members being lawyers! Doubtless it was with a wistful nostalgia that Oscar Wilde, in his memorable essay on *The Decay of Lying*, recalled this club and invented the 'Tired Hedonists ... to wear faded roses in our button-holes when we meet, and to have a sort of cult for Domitian'. Wilde's lament was that one of the chief causes of the 'curiously commonplace character of most of the literature of our age is undoubtedly the decay of lying as an art, a science and a social pleasure'. Wilde would have loved the golden age of clubmanship and one can picture him starting the Tired Hedonists in some cupid-canopied, marble folly and telling his polished and impossible stories to an enthralled gathering.

To appreciate fully the reasons for this passion for club life one must understand that it marked the birth pangs of the Romantic Movement in Britain. The seventeenth century had been one of bawdy, brawling and nauseating brutality which not even its veneer of sophisticated manners could disguise. A reaction from this was long overdue, and it took the form of a passion for style. Many factors had been at work to bring about the first glimmerings of Romance. The Goncourts wrote: 'The century has embraced the realities; it has restored activity to the senses; it has done away with sham and affectation.' This may not sound like the birth pangs of romanticism, but one must remember that this wasn't Daphnis and Chloe experiencing romance through innocence; it was worldly wise men sniffing out the dangers of the romantic spirit before they sampled it. The rakes learned the joys of romance the hard way. Their education, carefully rounded off by the Grand Tour, taught them early on that Romance may call from the hilltops to invoke the early riser in the name of beauty, but that it brings with her an incongruous and unseemly retinue.

There is her consort, Mephistopheles, her maid, Mischievousness, and her Ticket Collector, Love. But they were practical men. They did not sermonize about tedious and uninspiring stones, nor were they led astray by so utterly depraved a bird as the cuckoo, as was William Wordsworth a century later. They approached Romance, as they saw her in Italy, as uninhibited hedonists, yet taking care to guard their choicest discoveries by preserving a certain amount of awe. They realized that while life might be lived joyously and rumbustuously, it contained an element of melancholy and mystery that was worth nurturing. So they sought to have the best of both worlds – the world of carnal carnival and bachannalian revelry against a background of wild grandeur and Poesque grotesqueries. It was romance as it might be practised by Jean-Paul Sartre, should the founder of Existentialism ever seek to found a new school in the romantic mood.

The Grand Tour awakened in its participants a sense of the artistic liberalism of the Continent. The young men who made the Tour paid more attention to Italy than to France, though this was counterbalanced by the fact that for many of them Voltaire was the patron saint. They sharpened their intellect on the hard-headed logic of Latin rather than softening it up on the panegyrics of Greek. Similarly, those who went farther afield were more impressed by Turkey than by Greece. This enabled them to develop an outlook which was probably more suitable for their age than if they had cavorted down the emotion-tossed, primrose path to Athens.

A healthy native scepticism allied to a distaste for humbug caused them to enjoy Italy without allowing the romantic mood to turn them to religion. Indeed, these rakes were essentially radical in their outlook, whether Whig or Tory, and the very smell of incense or the least whisper of Papism was enough to incite them to blasphemy. Fear of the Roman Church was deep-rooted, and perhaps out of perversity, perhaps to ensure that their romantic urges were directed safely away from Rome, they took the keenest interest in occultism and black magic, which then flourished in many parts of Italy.

In the eighteenth century the squire and his eldest son came into their own. It is not exaggerating too much to assert that they were the vital force in England. In national affairs and in local government the role they filled was of tremendous importance. Squires like Harley, Walpole, Carteret, the Grenvilles and Francis Dashwood all achieved high office and great influence. Macaulay wrote that at this period 'the modern country gentleman generally receives a liberal education, passes from a distinguished school to a distinguished college, and has ample opportunity to become an excellent scholar. He has generally seen something of foreign countries. A considerable part of his life has been passed in the Capital; and the refinements of the Capital follow him into the country. There is perhaps no class of dwellings so pleasing as the rural seats of the English gentry. In the buildings, good sense and good taste combine to produce a happy union of the comfortable and the graceful.'

The Grand Tour gave to the sons of squires an appreciation of culture that had not previously been known in the English countryside. The squires of the beginning of the century were little better than farmers in their tastes and manners. They lived to hunt and to till. They improved their lands, but failed lamentably to improve their minds. But their sons changed all that. After the Grand Tour they took back to England a passion for Italian architecture. But what seemed aesthetically right in Italy did not fit into the English pattern of life. These young men sensed the need for a more sympathetic background to the Palladian column and statuary which they sought to reproduce in the slumbrous shires. To them rusticity was synonymous with domesticity and they felt that neither provided the right environment for the Italianate. Thus began a soon-to-be-fashionable cult for making gardens resemble nature in the raw. A garden, they decided, must not be a cosy, neat domestic paradise, but a broad splash of rugged grandeur, a landscape that had the wildness of a Scottish moor, a plot of ground that could be converted into acres of hillocks dotted with artificially contrived ruins, giving an atmosphere of genteel decay. It has been argued that these young patrons of the arts were anticipating Wordsworth. But, as we have already seen, they were too logical for that. They possessed none of Wordsworth's combination of narrow Anglicanism and romantic pantheism. Instead they tempered their romantic enthusiasms with agnosticism.

The truth was that Italy had given them a taste not only for Palladian architecture, but for romantic love. The blend of the two led them to believe that love-making required a new background. The pleasure gardens of Ranelagh and Vauxhall were all right for Roaring Boys to indulge their crude seductions and hoydenish flirtations, but serious wooing demanded a more secluded setting, remote from the mob, somewhere that exuded exoticism. So it was with one eye on creating a seduction ground that, with the aid of 'Capability' Brown and other artist-gardeners, they turned their country estates into a cross between the House of Usher and Wuthering Heights, a Heathcliffian blend of artificial mountains, lonely moors and decayed ruins. Nor was such horticulture a haphazard affair: in 1742 Batty Langley published his *Gothic Architecture improved by Rules and Proportions in many Grand Designs*, a work which was intended as a guide to the new school of garden designer who wished to lavish on his wild landscapes, grottoes, follies and ruins. An illustration in this book shows a plan for the construction of a hut, lined with trees, 'intended to represent the primitive state of the Dorick Order'.

Soon gardens ceased to be formal and their designers slavishly copied nature, eschewing the geometrical patterns beloved by an earlier age and making miniature mountains where there had been flower beds, ivied ruins in place of box hedges, waterfalls and pools, precipices and caves. The artistic wilderness became an ideal; an atmosphere of gloom and melancholy heightened the sense of remoteness and mystery. And amidst all this they built their follies, their enchanting frescoes and Tuscan columns, their catacombs (bringing nostalgia for Rome) and temples of Venus. Even Latin was revered because it added to the sense of style and drama. Even in pursuit of the bawdy the rake-gardeners never shirked the task of putting their naughty ditties into Latin verse.

But this quest for the proper setting for their grandiose fantasies in stone did not degenerate into an effete intellectualism. They approached art and literature in the manner of schoolboys delighting in a new toy, rounding off a piece of smut into an exquisite carving in stone, and avoiding all that was abstract and pretentious. In no way was the aura of mystery and melancholy which pervaded their estates allowed to colour their approach to life. This was not art for art's sake, but art for life's sake, and though these art-minded rakes had shared the Grand Tour and a classical education, the real bond between them was as often as not their devotion to the twin pursuits of Bacchus and Venus. They borrowed from Nature without mistaking Nature for Art, as did Wordsworth. If they had written odes to the cuckoo, they would not have talked of 'visionary hours', but would probably have composed a satire in Aristophanean vein on the parasitical decadence of the bird.

The passion for melancholic backgrounds might be compared with *fin de siècle*. The fascination for occultism, the quest for *un nouveau frisson* may suggest a parallel with the jaded dilettanti of the eighteen-nineties. . . .

> 'Pretty boys, witty boys, too, too, too
> Lazy to fight stagnation,
> Haughty boys, naughty boys, all we do
> Is to pursue sensation.'

But the rakes of the eighteenth century never permitted their devotion to art to make them unpractical or otherworldly. There was nothing precious about them. Melancholia was an affectation which did not affect their recreations. Rather did the grandiloquence of Palladian columns set against a garden that resembled an overgrown, neglected and bankrupt estate stimulate them to a greater reverence for their more venal activities. Dr. Samuel Johnson summed up this attitude when he claimed that they felt it necessary in their quest for women 'to represent themselves as undergoing every species of anguish which they suppose has been experienced by illustrious prototypes of love'.

It may be argued that it is wrong to keep referring to the rake-ruler class as 'they'. Surely, one may ask, these men were individualists and varied tremendously in opinions and outlook. While the answer is in the affirmative, it cannot be denied that there was a remarkable uniformity about them. It was this uniformity which their passion for club life induced. Few, if any, of these young men did not belong to some club or other, and membership gave them a common outlook. The rake of this period had become conscious of the need for some organization in his quest for pleasure. He had outgrown the crudities of earlier generations when the Roaring Boys terrorized whole neighbourhoods and kidnapped respectable housewives, rolling them down the streets in barrels – 'matrons poop'd in hogsheads', as Gay so aptly put it.

So the fastidious rake slowly took the place of the boasting, prattling, empty-headed Roaring Boy. He became more selective in his choice of companions, less willing to tolerate noisy bores, even seeking friends among the middle-class intelligentsia which was just emerging. And selective companionship was more easily achieved by forming clubs than by wandering from tavern to tavern in drunken, marauding bands.

Puritanically minded historians have made much foolish condemnation of the eighteenth-century rake. The portrait of a dissolute, hard-drinking, profane and lecherous society is merely one side of the coin. On the reverse is a very different picture, revealing that, by and large, the rake of this period was a more honest man than his Victorian counterpart, less empty-headed than the Edwardian masher (perhaps the nadir of rakemanship), club-minded, yet imaginative and individualistic, a progressive landlord, a patron of arts, politically active and a cultured and knowledgeable fellow. Whatever his faults and excesses, his vices and political chicaneries, he was a man who had a social conscience more often than not and one who helped to make history. At the worst he may have been an amoral politician, or a third-rate statesman, but it is to his credit that he not only tippled, but found time to govern, not only devoted himself to the arts of seduction, but toppled the nobility from their perch as arbiters of the nation's destiny.

Doubtless the literary traditions of the coffee and chocolate houses contributed to the spirit of clubmanship, but, as the country squires and their sons outnumbered the literary men, so they set the tone to the new clubs. And the half-understood spirit of romanticism which they brought from the Continent was an even more vital factor. They began to organize their devotions to Bacchus and Venus into a club ritual. Formal dinners, with toasts to Bacchus, and sonnets specially composed for the occasion took the place of spontaneous, drunken orgies. As for seduction, the new method was to escape from the crowd, to practise their talents in their own lonely gardens and in man-made caves. Instead of wenching in the taverns, they would hold week-end orgies for club members on their own estates, or in private rooms at club headquarters. And those of the young bloods who had included Turkey in their Grand Tour borrowed ideas of oriental splendour and set up harems for themselves.

Indeed, Turkey appealed to this generation as Greece did to the Byronic Age which was to follow. The passion for harems led to the setting up of private bordellos. The Divan Club, which met at the Thatched Tavern in St. James's Street, was a direct result of Turkish influence. Its members wore daggers and turbans when they dined.

Travelling in Italy had brought about a craze for paganism as well as the classics and a realization that the Englishman's reputation as a lover was far from high on the Continent. He was regarded as stiff and boorish, clumsy in his amorous approaches. The truth was that for more than half a century seduction had been too easy for him. The ruling classes had been getting their own way without having to exercise any technique. They had not had to contend with the agents of the Inquisition like Casanova and lack of opposition makes Cupid a dull dog.

London's morals were probably the loosest in Europe. Easy virtue had become a bore. So, to be really *à la mode*, the new fashion was to set love-making on a more grandiose, if not a higher plane. But the reason why the age failed to produce any notable romantic lovers in England was that clubmanship called for team work rather than individual efforts at seduction. There were few 'lone wolves', few attempts at romantic monogamy. Seduction was a sport to be shared, analysed and duly debated by club members. It was generally, though not always, accepted that marriage was a matter of financial arrangements convenient to both parties, and that sexual adventure was to be sought outside the sphere of matrimony. There was a juvenile attitude to this quest for adventure, and club members not only compared notes and exchanges mistresses, but kept lists of approved harlots, with detailed memoranda of their qualities and foibles. These were exchanged within a limited circle.

Romantics though they might have been, they had a mania for comparing notes both verbally and by letter on their sexual escapades and were always giving one another advice. Thus John Wilkes, writing to his friend, Charles Churchill, the poet, enjoined him that 'you should not fail to make yourself known to Effie when at Tunbridge Wells. By all means mention my name and you will find her both pliant and pliable. She is gifted with a capacity for translating the language of love into a rich, libidinous and ribald phraseology which lends enchantment to her amoristic acrobatics.'

The Society for the Propagation of Sicilian Amorology contained in its records these notes on its 'feminine accessories': 'Antonina, Priscilla and Evadne have this day passed the most rigorous tests of the Brotherhood and have been accepted as Sisters according to the laws of the Society. I hereby testify that they are virgins all and have been instructed in the arts and sciences in which they will be expected to give satisfaction to members. Signed, Brother Tiberius.'

Even so sedate a scholar as Benjamin Franklin was sufficiently the child of his age, when in England, to write

22

these words of advice to an acquaintance who was cogitating whether to seek a mistress. While urging that matrimony was undoubtedly the ideal state, Franklin suggested that if his friend must take a mistress he should avoid young virgins, but seek 'a discreet and older woman': . . . 'because in every animal that walks upright, the deficiency of the fluids that fill the muscles appears first in the highest part, the face. Covering all above with a basket and regarding only what is below the girdle, it is impossible of two women to know an old one from a young one. And as in the dark all cats are grey, the pleasure of corporal enjoyment with an old woman is at least equal, and frequently superior.'

Meanwhile many clubs specialized in copying pagan ritual on their convivial evenings. There was the Sunday Night Club, which practised corybantic orgies, and occultism was occasionally introduced to heighten the atmosphere and relieve the monotony. It has already been explained that visits to Italy, while producing a love of classicism and paganism, also inspired a revolt against Papist customs. This revolt became so intense that it developed into an aesthetic reaction against anything that smacked of Rome, and clubs sprang up which prided themselves on their blasphemousness and vied with one another in sneering at religion. There was a spate of clubs bearing the name 'Hell-Fire', one of the most prominent of which was founded in 1720 by Lord Wharton (later the Duke of Wharton). A menu of this club included in its dishes 'Hell Fire Punch', 'Holy Ghost Pye', 'Devil's Loins' and 'Breast of Venus', the latter being two pullets arranged to resemble a woman's breasts and garnished with cherries for nipples.

On 28 April, 1721, a royal proclamation was issued against 'blasphemous clubs in London', and for another twenty years nothing more was heard of them. In the late 'twenties of the century the tone of clubs tended to change again, and the emphasis was on ritualistic dinners, patronage of the arts and dressing up in oriental costumes. There was the Sublime Society of Beefsteaks, which met each Sunday at the top of Covent Garden Theatre, of which

John Wilkes was a member, and the Dilettanti Society in 1732, devoted to 'eating, drinking and discussing the arts'.

Once again members became more selective in their choice of feminine society, though judging from the correspondence of Boswell, Wilkes, Churchill, Lord Sandwich and others, this does not seem to have saved them from the dangers inherent in promiscuity. They were for ever telling each other of their venal casualties. Bluntly Lord Sandwich told John Wilkes: 'You will either die from the pox, or be hanged.' To which Wilkes spontaneously replied: 'That depends on whether I embrace your principles or your mistress.'

But more often the rakes referred to their ailments in a roundabout way – *'Monsieur la croix de Venus'*, or 'Signor Gonorrhoea'.

Tiring of the lists of harlots which were circulated among club members (one club actually printed a *Guide to a Whoremonger's London*) the young rakes advertised for amorous adventures. The newspapers of the period contained many examples of this. . . .

'Wanted. A Woman in the poet's sense with a capital W. With soft lips, expressive eyes, sweet breath, bosom full and plump, firm and white, lively conversation and one looking as if she could feel delight where she wishes to give it.'

Yet, 'romantic melancholy swept the country', wrote one author of the period. It was a gross exaggeration. The 'melancholy' was reserved for the new-style gardens and for mutual commiseration after hard-drinking bouts and when recovering from some venal ailment. In the club rooms gaiety was cherished above all else, and second to that wit. At the King's Head in Pall Mall it was the custom of the World Club that members should write epigrams on the wine glasses. Edward Young, author of *Night Thoughts*, who laid no claim to be a wit, begged to be excused on the grounds that he possessed no diamond with which to write. However, the excuse was disallowed, and Lord Stanhope promptly lent him his own diamond with which Young scrawled:

'Accept a miracle instead of wit –
See two dull lines with Stanhope's pencil writ.'

By the 'forties clubmen were becoming weary of formal gatherings and the desire for some new element of sensation to titillate their jaded palates made itself felt. Among the older clubmen there was much sighing for the old-time orgies of the Hell-Fire clubs, but no one dared to revive them until Sir Francis Dashwood surreptitiously founded the Brotherhood of 'Saint Francis of Wycombe'. Perhaps it was a whim with a double purpose when he gave the new club this name; at least it sought to disguise the real activities of the 'Brothers'. Though history and legend has re-named this organization the 'Hell-Fire Club', the title was never used by any of its members. Only towards the end of the eighteenth century and in the early nineteenth, when its exploits were publicized, did this name come to be adopted. No contemporary figure ever referred to it as such, though the Brothers were variously mentioned as 'The Monks of Medmenham', 'The Medmenham Friars', 'The Franciscans', 'The Order of Saint Francis', and 'Dashwood's Apostles'.

Doubtless the club was often confused with the original Hell-Fire clubs like that founded by Lord Wharton. Nevertheless, in popular legend it remains the most notorious society ever to be formed in Britain and has been painted in truly satanic colours. Gossip and wild tittle-tattle about Dashwood and his followers grew with the years, and in the early nineteenth century Hell-Fire clubs were formed in places as far apart as Dublin, Edinburgh and Paris, while in 1828, a society modelled on the Franciscans was started at Brasenose College, Oxford.

A North Country version of the Brotherhood was formed by John Hall Stevenson, a friend of Sterne, and the author of a Rabelaisian collection of fables and verse published under the title of *Crazy Tales* in 1772. This society was named the Demoniacs and there is evidence that Dashwood was consulted and asked for his advice on the rituals which it should adopt. But the Demoniacs never achieved the same fame as the Franciscans, nor did their bogus ruined castle in Yorkshire attract members as illustrious as those who gathered first at Medmenham Abbey and later in the caves beneath West Wycombe Hill.

For it is not surprising that the Brotherhood should have become a lurid legend. Its members included at least one Prime Minister, a Chancellor of the Exchequer, a First Lord of the Admiralty, various Cabinet Ministers, a Lord Mayor of London, a general and an Oxford professor, not to mention two or three of the best-known poets of the day and in Hogarth the age's greatest satirical painter. So the myth arose in the twilight of Victorian prudery that in the previous century England had been ruled by a gaggle of wicked, satanically minded rakes from chalk caves cut deep into the heart of a Buckinghamshire hill.

Fact had been twisted into fantasy by eighteenth-century denigrators of the club. The Victorians, aghast at anything that smacked of pagan ritual, nevertheless made pilgrimages up the Thames to Medmenham and the Ferry Boat Inn became a rendezvous for touts who would further shock their visitors with gruesome tales of obscene rites practised by hooded 'monks' in the ruined abbey. The caves, however, remained more or less forgotten for many years. By the end of the nineteenth century both Medmenham and West Wycombe had ceased to draw the crowds. It was not until 1952, that Mr. Francis Dashwood, a descendant of Sir Francis's half-brother[1] and son of the present baronet, Sir John Dashwood, reopened the caves at West Wycombe and revived the title of the Hell-Fires Caves.

Once again the English fondness for a picturesque and devilish rake was manifested, and so today thousands of people go down to Buckinghamshire and pay two shillings to explore the still eerie quarter mile of twisting passages and caves where the Franciscans conducted their club rituals. The receipts go towards the cost of repairing various ancient and historic buildings at West Wycombe.

One can be sure that Sir Francis would thoroughly approve of this.

1. Sir John Dashwood-King.

CHAPTER 2

LEGEND, coloured by puritanical prejudice and sheer sensationalism, has not been kind to the founder of the Order of 'Saint' Francis.

Whig historians have depicted him as one of the blackest scoundrels of his age, and those who have attempted to chronicle his life have not erased this portrait. They have unfairly concentrated on one aspect of this remarkable man's career with the result that 'Hell-Fire Francis' is the epithet by which he is still most generally known.

It has been said that Max Beerbohm had Sir Francis Dashwood in mind when he created the character of Lord George Hell in his 'fairy tale for tired men', that exquisite romance, *The Happy Hypocrite*. If so, Beerbohm was kinder than most for, while showing the 'wicked' side of Lord George's character, he did not omit the redeeming features. And, taking this story as a moral, in retrospect Sir Francis was no worse and a great deal better than some of his contemporaries.

Born in 1708, he could claim an indirect relationship to John Milton, for a descendant of one of the poet's daughters married his half-brother. Perhaps this family link is no more incongruous than the fact that the author of *Paradise Lost* could also write about 'pert fairies and dapper elves'. Francis was the second baronet, the only son of his father's second marriage to Mary Fane, eldest daughter and eventually co-heiress of Vere, fourth Earl of Westmorland. He was a likeable and personable youth, who succeeded to the baronetcy at the age of sixteen. Fortune smiled on him at this early age. Not only did he inherit a large estate both in land and cash, but he enjoyed the very best education a young man could have at this time. The conventional classical education of the day at Charterhouse was rounded off by the Grand Tour of the Continent, the customary finishing course for scions of the aristocracy.

Francis has been portrayed as squandering his youth in riotous living and 'fornicating his way across Europe'. According to one source, he 'joined the Hell-Fire Club in 1725'. This last statement is manifestly absurd. In 1725 he was only seventeen years old and he could hardly have been carrying out a prolonged tour of Europe and indulging in orgies at home at the same time. In any event by 1721 the edict banning all Hell-Fire clubs had come into force, and, precocious though he may have been, it is unlikely that he would have had the opportunity of joining such a club at the age of twelve. But this is but one of many allegations designed to show him up in an unfavourable light. Certainly he played the rake, but in the National Trust version of the history of West Wycombe House, the Dashwood country seat in Buckinghamshire, it is stated that 'posterity has somewhat unfairly woven an exaggerated notoriety round his personality, on account of his pronounced animal spirits'. This seems to be a necessary qualification in assessing his character.

Though there is little trace of many of his continental escapades, some of the major incidents of his Grand Tour days have been recorded. In his youth he had a passion for travel much in excess of that of most of his compatriots. He visited Russia and is said to have masqueraded at St. Petersburg as Charles XII of Sweden, the great adversary of Peter the Great. But as Charles had been dead for many years, one cannot altogether accept this version by Walpole of what happened at the Russian court. It would be in keeping with his fondness for amorous adventure that he used this disguise to seduce the Tsarina Anne, a liaison which is said to have been maintained for some months. But one must sometimes take Walpole's statements guardedly. He seems to have been both fascinated and repulsed by Dashwood, noting the latter's numerous love affairs in France and Italy, and commenting tartly and perhaps even jealously, 'he has the staying power of a stallion and the impetuosity of a bull'.

Walpole, though usually factually correct, was not always

a reliable witness and was apt to be primly waspish about people he did not like. He detested Dashwood and his pen recorded his prejudices. He found him 'seldom sober', yet grudgingly admitted that he possessed 'charm, tolerance and frankness'. Wraxhall went so far as to assert that Francis Dashwood 'far exceeded in licentiousness of conduct anything exhibited since Charles II's reign'.

On the other hand R. Gibbs, author of *Worthies of Buckinghamshire*, quotes Dr. Bates, of Amersham and Edinburgh, an acquaintance of Dashwood's over a long period, as 'repeatedly' declaring that Sir Francis was 'a man of unimpeachable honour'. Perhaps Dr Bates was too close a friend to have formed an unbiased opinion, but there is ample other testimony to Dashwood's frankness and honesty. William Pitt the Elder admired the Squire of West Wycombe for 'being so honest as to speak his mind'. Henry Fox wrote to the Earl of Bute, saying 'Dashwood is an honest man and he has the best intentions'. George Prescott wrote to Dashwood that 'persons of your resolution, ability and honesty are more than ever necessary in the Departments of State'.

In sifting through the correspondence of the period in the Egerton Manuscripts in the British Museum one finds these tributes so often that it is impossible not to revise the narrow, stereotyped view of the man as a half-witted rake. 'You have more justice and humanity than I,' wrote Barrington, and Dr William King, principal of St. Mary Hall, Oxford, a shrewd judge of men and no sycophant, proffered to Dashwood the congratulations of 'an old recluse who loves and honours you and who, without the gift of prophecy, can foretell that a few gentlemen of your character placed about a young king will make him as well as his people easy and happy'.

Even John Wilkes, despite his political castigations of Dashwood and his confrères, often referred to his 'rare gifts of imagination and very real mental abilities'. Indeed Wilkes owed much of his own advance to the Squire of West Wycombe, handsomely acknowledging that, 'It shall always be my endeavour to merit the obliging things you are so kind to say of me.'

This trait of honesty of mind is one to which friend and foe alike paid tribute. It was, perhaps, one of the few virtues of Dashwood's dissolute companion during the Grand Tour – the notorious Earl of Sandwich, noted for the astonishing contrast of his extreme ugliness of countenance and charmingly ingratiating manners. Both men cared nothing for what other people thought or said, and made a point of expressing bluntly whatever was in their minds. Sandwich had married Judith, daughter of Viscount Fane, a relative of Dashwood's mother. This pair of mischievous rakes visited Turkey together, and it was on their suggestion that the Divan Club made the wearing of turbans at its functions a condition of membership. Alas, the minutes of the Divan Club, though they still exist, give no clue to its proceedings or amusements, though 'The Harem' was a regular toast at its dinners and may hint at the most obvious recreation of its members. The latter were recognized by oriental titles, Sir Francis being known as 'El Faquir Dashwood Pasha'.

While making his tour Francis certainly did not neglect his studies, not merely under the prompting of a tutor for whom he seems to have had the greatest contempt, but on his own initiative as well. He took a lively and even erudite interest in the places he visited. He was fascintated by the classical ruins of Italy and made detailed investigations of many of them. Proof of this interest lies in the fact that he delivered a paper on the subject to the Dilettanti Club, which he helped to found in 1732.[1] The members of the society were mostly hard-drinking rakes, but they did not warrant the stricture of Walpole to Horace Mann in 1743: 'The Dilettanti, a club for which the nominal qualification is having been to Italy, but the real one being drunk. The two chiefs are Lord Middlesex and Sir Francis Dashwood, who were seldom sober the whole time they were in Italy.'

The members of the Dilettanti took themselves sufficiently seriously to devote much time to studying classical art. Sir Francis was primarily responsible for this club producing the first important study of classical ruins – *The*

1. 'If not the actual projector and founder of the Dilettanti, he was certainly its leading member.' (Cust.)

Antiquities of Athens, carried out by James Stuart and Nicholas Revett. In addition, again at Dashwood's prompting, the society sent members to Rome, both architects and young artists, and a direct result of their efforts was the excavations at Herculaneum in 1738, which was followed by those at Pompeii ten years later.

West Wycombe House had been the home of the Dashwood family since 1698, when Thomas Lewis, an alderman of the City of London, made over the property to two of his wife's brothers. The elder, Samuel, became Lord Mayor of London, while the younger, Francis, when created a baronet in 1707, bought out his brother's interest and settled at West Wycombe. Young Francis had always had ideas of developing the estate and bringing about an architectural renaissance in the neighbourhood. It was with this idea in mind that he spent much of his time on the Continent in the company of architects and artists, sculptors and designers.

Back from his travels he devoted his attentions to his estate and his tenants. His architectural achievements deserve a chapter on their own, but inasmuch as they throw light on his character, it is essential to pay tribute to his most obvious gift to posterity. He had a genuine flair for architecture and it was not merely a slavish imitation of the Italianate; he possessed the imagination to adapt Italian ideas to the English countryside and to add to them something of his own love of the fantastic. In some ways he was an eighteenth century Lord Berners. He built the present West Wycombe House and made it one of the finest examples of Palladian artistry in Britain with its three hundred feet double colonnade and exquisitely wrought frescoes. But it was his genius for providing the right background to his artistic creations, his flair for putting oddities in the wrong place and getting away with them by sheer artistic instinct which enabled him to squeeze the maximum effect from his work.

Nor was he simply copying current fashions. He was a pioneer in the architectural field at a time when neither Italian nor Greek art had become fashionable in England. To the Chiltern Hills he brought a handsome villa which might well have been transplanted from some Italian plain and strewed his gardens with Greek and Roman temples. Most of this building took place between 1745 and 1771. He selected the best talent to put his ideas into being – Nicholas Revett, his Dilettanti Club companion, Robert Adam, John Donowell and, later, Atterbury.

In his quest for nature in the raw he converted his estate into a singularly attractive, if rather sinister blend of wildness and beauty, and dotted about this untamed landscape were frolics and minuets in stone which bewitched and captivated visitors by their pagan loveliness. Thomas Langley in *The History of Antiquities of the Hundred of Desborough* wrote, 'the character of the place is beauty; there is nothing grand or sublime, but the whole scene is cheerful and animated. The water, whether divided into several streams expanding into a clear, pellucid lake, or meandering in a gentle river through the lawn, is the leading feature of the landscape.'

And Benjamin Franklin, who later became his great friend, made this comment in a letter to his son in America, written from West Wycombe in 1773: 'I am in this house as much at my ease as if it was my own; and the gardens are a paradise. But a pleasanter thing is the kind countenance, the facetious and very intelligent conversation of Mine Host, who, having been for many years engaged in public affairs, seen all parts of Europe, and kept the best company in the world, is himself the best existing.'

This is a very different picture from that drawn by Ronald Fuller,[1] who wrote of Dashwood's 'arrested intellectual development – fixed at the mental age of about eighteen'.

Francis was an incredible mixture of Radical-Tory – a Tory cocktail with a dash of Jacobinism and a generous measure of Radical spirits. This statement may seem irreconcilable. Yet, he could, while detesting Catholicism and loathing Popery, make friends with Catholics. A Tory by instinct, he was nevertheless never an uncompromising party man and often showed a streak of individualism in his politics. In his youth he wrote republican and anti-court sentiments in verse. These may have been the fleeting whims of a young man, but his reputation as a dangerous republi-

1. *Hell-Fire Francis,* by Ronald Fuller.

can was such that Frederick, Prince of Wales, once told him: 'You would make me the greatest *Stadtholder* England ever had.'

Such political idiosyncrasies are not so rare a phenomenon as they may seem in this twentieth century. The true Tory, as distinct from the commercialized and retreating Conservative into which his descendants have mostly degenerated, has always had a *soupçon* of radicalism in his make-up. He is a romanticist, a mystic-royalsit and a democrat, and often he is far more capable of smoking out and imbibing the romanticism of radicalism than politicians of the doctrinal left. It is interesting to note that Lord Sandwich's descendant, Lord Hinchingbrooke, is in this tradition and one of the few practising examples today of Toryism in its most honest expression.

Sir Francis shared some of John Wilkes's advanced ideas and was a wholehearted admirer of Voltaire, whose works he studied diligently. Yet, while in Rome, he developed a romantic enthusiasm for the Young Pretender, and made the acquaintance of Prince Charles Edward. Indeed, Horace Mann sent home reports complaining of Dashwood's 'subversive activities as a Jacobin agent', alleging that he had written to the Pretender's court, telling them that the British Prime Minister was about to fall. But Mann, like Walpole, is not always to be relied upon. As a secret agent he sent home the kind of reports he thought his masters would wish to read. Mann tried to paint the Young Pretender as a 'moral and physical wreck', a report which was certainly belied in the '45 Rebellion and is hardly credible when one realizes that Charles Edward lived until he was sixty-eight and never had a breakdown in health until his very last days.

The Dashwood family had Jacobite sympathies and it is highly probable that the comparative elegance and graciousness of the exiled Prince's court made a pleasant contrast to the grossness and Teutonic awkwardness of that of the Georges. In the late 'thirties Dashwood seems to have played with the idea of throwing in his lot with the Jacobites and he paid a second visit to Italy, during which he supplied the Prince with certain information. But the information provided was that of a warm-hearted friend reporting on conditions at home; it was never subversive, as Mann suggested, nor was it a breach of the laws. At this period – round about 1740 – he made the acquaintance of Lady Mary Wortley-Montagu in Florence and she may well have been concerned in all this.

Ultimately the common sense in Dashwood's make-up must have warned him against such a romantic attachment in politics. He told the Earl of Sandwich: 'I am at one with this gallant Prince. He has all the gifts of a true leader and above all he is honest. But I detest most heartily the fripperies of Rome which emanate from his entourage. He will never join the Papists, but that hypocritical bunch of candle-burners would be unwelcome over here, and, should the Prince truly come into his own, it is difficult to see how he could keep away from their influence.'

In January 1751 Dashwood made a rather ostentatious disavowal of Jacobitism. This was perhaps forced on him by reason of the intrigues of Mann and the suspicion, quite unfounded, that he and other Tories were plotting with the Prince.

Meanwhile, gossip-loving Walpole followed Dashwood's amatory exploits as closely in England as in Rome or St. Petersburg. In a letter which Walpole wrote on 29 May, 1744, he said: 'Dashwood (Lady Carteret's *quondam* lover) has stolen a great fortune, a Miss Bateman.' The statement was a little premature, for no match was made.

Back at home after his travels, Dashwood was a forthright champion of commoners' rights, while, not unnaturally, taking every measure to safeguard his own. 'The parishioners,' he wrote, 'will keep what they want, which is the wood, and Sir Francis Dashwood will not lose the privilege of hunting and shooting and his right of game as far as his manor extends.'

Macaulay has described the household of the ordinary country squires of the age as 'the litter of a farm-yard gathered under the windows of his bed-chamber, and the cabbages and gooseberry bushes grew close to his hall door'. This is not an exaggerated picture; there are other contemporary accounts of the manor houses of the eighteenth century which reveal that many squires differed little from yeomen farmers. They paid no rent, they had ample grazing grounds and their meat, venison, game, fish, eggs, butter and milk were produced on their own land. With agriculture becoming more prosperous they had every chance to provide better standards for their tenants and themselves. But it was mainly the educated and wealthy squires – men like Dashwood and Thomas Coke, the man who turned Norfolk into a rich and fertile region and raised the profits of his tenants – who attempted this.

At the end of the 'forties there was a famine in many areas of Britain and consequently much unemployment. Sir Francis, by no means indifferent to the social problems of the age, realized that failure to do anything about this could only bring discontent and possibly revolution. Determined that in Buckinghamshire the problem of unemployment should be tackled, he created in 1750 a new road from the Bird in Hand Inn to the village of West Wycombe to take the place of the rough track which ran alongside the wall of West Wycombe Park. 'My sole reason for making it was the welfare of the villagers,' he declared. 'I am determined that they should have employment.'

His enemies always alleged that the building of a road was a mere excuse for excavating the Hell-Fire Caves under West Wycombe Hill. They pointed out that the chalk used to make the present main road between West Wycombe and High Wycombe came from tunnelling operations under the hill. So, they argue, the road building was really a camouflage for the main operation. The road was completed in 1752 by the erection of an obelisk which still stands at its junction with the Aylesbury road, bearing the testimony, 'Sir F. Dashwood *derae Christianae* MDCCLII.'

Excavations probably began about 1748, but it is doubtful if the caves were finished before the end of 1752 at the earliest. Even if they were completed by that date, they were certainly not the headquarters of the Brotherhood until much later. It is likelier that the idea of utilizing the excavations for such a purpose was an afterthought. But indisputably the excavations provided the materials for a much-needed road, while the men who carved out the caves entirely by hand were the unemployed of the district, who received one shilling per head in payment.

Painters of the period, notably Knapton and Hogarth, are largely responsible for Dashwood's portrayal as a debauched, crazy creature. Knapton painted him in the habit of a friar, tonsured, with wineglass in hand, gazing at a miniature statue of a naked Venus, while round his head was a halo bearing the legend *San Francesco di Wycombo*. It is really a cartoon portrait, as, too, was Hogarth's interpretation. Nathaniel Dance also painted him as 'Saint' Francis with all the paraphernalia of satanic imagery, even to the extent of a skull in one corner of the picture. The best portrait is that executed by the French artist, Carpentiers. It shows the Squire of West Wycombe as round-faced, rather pensive, yet kindly and humorous and not at all vicious of countenance. This, according to those who knew him, was a realistic picture, and for this reason one can discount the many obscene caricatures drawn by Hogarth and others.

Politics actively claimed Dashwood's attention in 1741, when, at the age of thirty-three, he became Member of Parliament for Romney, a seat he held until 1761. It cannot be too markedly emphasized that politics brought him many enemies and that the smears on his character were mostly political in origin. This particularly applies in the case of Horace Walpole, whose father Sir Robert was the Whig *eminence grise* of the day and deplorably given to the abuse of patronage. Since the Revolution of 1688 the two-party system had dominated British politics. That there was chicanery at the highest level is not to be denied, but the two-party system had at least the safeguard that no party could hope to remain in power unless it carried with it the majority of voters. Despite the system of 'pocket boroughs' and a restricted electorate, this check of the will of the people did to a great extent work. The Whig Party remained in power for most of the time from 1688 to the end of George II's reign. The strength of the Whigs lay in their support in the larger towns and among the wealthy families; the Tories were backed by a majority of the smaller squires and had quite widespread encouragement from all classes of society. Throughout their long period in opposition they had considerable strength in parliament.

In practice not a great deal separated the two parties. In theory, however, and in the political speeches of the period such differences as there were became magnified into distortions which amounted to phobias. The Whigs ruled for so long because they were able to play on the fear of a majority of the people that the Tories were secretly Jacobites and against the House of Hanover. In fact, very few Tories took any such view. They had above all else a passion for law and order, an attachment to the monarchy and a conviction that the return of a Roman Catholic ruler would be disastrous for the nation.

There is very little documentary evidence as to how Toryism maintained its strength during this, the most barren period of its existence. But, just as the Conservative Party, after its shattering defeat in 1945, decided that it must destroy the legend that it was the party of privilege and the rich, so the leading Tories began to realize that the only way they could remove the suspicion that they were anti-Hanover was by coming out as a one hundred per cent pro-Royalist party.

The electorate had for years refused to believe their protestations of loyalty to the monarchy meant anything at all. So, gradually, by intricate manoeuvres, by forming a clique round the person of Frederick, Prince of Wales, who was popular with the masses, they appeared in the guise of the 'King's Friends', and later as supporters of George III's personal rule.

About a year after his election to Parliament, Dashwood began his lengthy association with one of the greatest Tory wirepullers of the era, George Bubb Dodington, wealthy Member of Parliament for Winchelsea, a neighbouring constituency to Dashwood's at Romney. Both men's London houses were in Pall Mall, and it was Dodington who introduced Dashwood to the circle of sycophants and political intriguers who surrounded the Prince of Wales.

Then, after the death of the Prince, Dodington courted Pelham, and for a while Dashwood was an intermediary between Pelham and Middlesex. Though never one of the sycophants in the royal circle, he was nevertheless quick to appreciate that the House of Hanover was throwing off its Teutonic prejudices and becoming progressively Anglicized. He was not a particularly successful Member of Parliament in the early years. During his first Parliament he took a distinctly independent line in the House of Commons, pressing for double taxation of 'placemen and pensioners', a policy which could by no stretch of imagination be said to be sycophantic. In 1745, he was urging the freeing of the Commons from 'undue influence', with hints of bribery in high places, and was a strong opponent of what he called 'the German war'. That streak of radicalism, which he never completely lost, was most marked in this period.

In 1745 he married a wealthy widow of Iver, Buckinghamshire, Sarah, Lady Ellis, whom Walpole sneeringly referred to as 'a poor, forlorn Presbyterian prude'. Dashwood has been represented as an indifferent and neglectful husband, and his enemies, such as Walpole and Wraxhall, sought to show that the marriage was 'an utter failure', claiming that the proof of this lay in the fact that there was no issue by it. Such a picture is simply untrue. Though physically unfaithful to Sarah, Francis was in his own way a loyal husband, and by eighteenth-century standards kinder and more sentimental than most. From 1767 until her death in 1769 he stayed with his wife and rarely left her company. He wrote to the Duke of Grafton: 'I have long since been a constant attendant upon the afflictions and uncommon distress of a woman, the worthiest and best friend any man ever had.' Many letters in similar strain were written by him to his wife, expressing his delight in her company and deep affection for her.

In 1760 the political scene underwent a change by the advent to the throne of George III. For the first time in the comparatively short history of the House of Hanover there was a king who was regarded by his subjects with something like enthusiasm. Twenty-three years old, handsome and popular, George III made a profound impression when in his first Speech from the Throne he declared: 'Born and educated in this country, I glory in the name of Britain, and the peculiar happiness of my life will ever consist, in promoting the welfare of my people, whose loyalty and warm affection to me, I consider as the greatest and most permanent security of my Throne.'

In 1761 Dashwood was elected M.P. for Weymouth and Melcombe Regis, and it is noteworthy that when Dodington became a peer he took the title of Lord Melcombe Regis.

But the reign that began so gloriously and with such expectations was speedily marred by the ganging-up of the Tories round the King. It would be true to say that there was no need for a 'King's Party' when George came to the throne. The creation of this was solely political expediency aimed at getting the Tories back into power. And so it was that in 1761 the Tories regained much lost ground, not as a Parliamentary party, but as supporters of George III's personal rule.

In 1762 the ill-fated Ministry of the Earl of Bute took office and Dashwood was appointed Chancellor of the Exchequer. It was a lamentable choice on the part of Bute and savoured of favouritism, for Dashwood had no inclination and no aptitude for such an office. He recorded that he had had 'a profound aversion to mathematics all my life. I am quite incapable of doing any sum which contains more than five figures.'

His first budget was received with hoots of laughter and much derision in the House of Commons. His financial statement was confused and absurd. It was said of him that at the Treasury he 'stumbled over farthings and trod lightly over pounds'. The poet, Charles Churchill, commented in verse . . .

> 'Dashwood shall pour, from a communion cup,
> Libations to the goddess without eyes,
> And hot or not in cider and excise.'

The 'goddess without eyes' was Angerona, the Egyptian goddess of silence which was to be found at Medmenham Abbey, and the reference was a castigation to Dashwood's proposal to place an excise duty on cider.

Yet the Chancellor was fully conscious of his limitations and too honest to try to disguise them. Indeed, his honesty on the occasion of his budget more than redeemed the situation. 'What shall I do?' he asked. 'The boys will point at me in the street and cry, "There goes the worst Chancellor of the Exchequer that ever was".'

George Grenville came to his rescue, and urged that the 'profusion with which the late war had been carried on made additional taxes necessary'. But Grenville's prolixity only made the situation more ludicrous, 'Tell me where you would have a tax laid?' asked Grenville. 'I say, sir, let them tell me where. I repeat it, sir, I am entitled to say, let them tell me where,' he whined.

Pitt threw the whole House into uproarious laughter to the complete discomfiture of the Government, by quoting in mocking whine resembling Grenville's the line of a well-known song, 'Gentle Shepherd, tell me where'. Then he bowed and walked out of the House. From then on Grenville was nicknamed 'The Gentle Shepherd'.

All the Tory squires in the cider-producing shires were up in arms against what they called the 'monstrous cider tax'. Certainly his budget contributed to the downfall of the Bute government, though there does not seem to be any evidence that he was unpopular with his colleagues. Dodington, in his diary of 6 February, 1761, referred to the possibility of 'Sir Francis Dashwood succeeding Charles Townshend as Secretary of State for War'.

In 1763 Dashwood was raised to the peerage as Lord le Despencer. On the death of his maternal uncle, the Earl of Westmorland, in that year, the ancient and premier barony of le Despencer lapsed into abeyance. But the barony was restored in Sir Francis's favour – 'to decorate his fall', John Wilkes maliciously remarked. But there is no gainsaying that Dashwood was much more honest than most of his colleagues. Elizabeth Montagu, the authoress and social leader, who was the friend of most of the notabilities of the day, wrote in a letter to a friend: 'The King told Sir Francis, when he gave him the seals, that he had a very good opinion of him, and was glad to have such an opportunity of showing it, that he has always heard he was an honest man, and, for his part, he desired to employ such.'

Political enemies sneered that the peerage for Dashwood was the worst kind of political favouritism and said that it was 'an act of jobbery' coming immediately after his political eclipse. Such sneers, however, were all part of the campaign to discredit the 'King's Friends' and there were many accusations of corruption and the selling of honours during 1763, largely arising out of the allegation that a sum of £25,000 had been paid out in pension and subsidies, bribes and gratuities to secure a majority for the Treaty of Paris, which was signed by Britain, France, Spain and Portugal. This was the treaty which virtually ended the Seven Years War.

Yet the sale of honours in the eighteenth century was never on anything like the scale which so discredited the Coalition Government of 1918–22. It was generally accepted that those who served the nation in Parliament had a claim on the funds of the State and should receive places of profit. Such emolument was regarded as a normal return for public services. George III had been loath to create too many new peers and the giving and receiving of honours were certainly not corrupt in most instances. Both the Whigs and the Tories made full use of the pocket boroughs – the small towns and villages which had the privilege of returning members of Parliament and where the local squire could influence the voting. What by the early nineteenth century had become an anachronistic form of corruption was in the mid-eighteenth century not such a bad thing in practice. In effect it meant that young men, as soon as they reached the age of twenty-one, could purchase a borough and get into Parliament. Those who had the money to do so had also had the benefits of the Grand Tour and a first-class education, and these were the vital factors which enabled so much talent to enter the House of Commons. By the time these young men had reached their thirties they were often, like Pitt, skilled and experienced administrators. Had there not been ample opportunities for youth to buy its way into Parliament, the Commons might have been stunted by representation from old-fashioned, stay-at-home squires who would have hung on to their seats until they were well past their dotage.

Dashwood's political allegiances did not prevent his seeking friends outside his party, and it was his companionship with such men as John Wilkes and Charles Churchill that helped to pave the way to his political downfall, as will be seen later. Referring to the association of Dashwood, Wilkes, the Earl of Sandwich, Charles Churchill and Robert Lloyd (all of whom were members of the Order of 'Saint' Francis), Walpole remarked that 'politics no sooner infused themselves amongst these rosy anchorites than their dissensions were kindled'. It was a fatal mistake to permit rival politicians to become members of this club, however great a tolerance this showed in its founder. Soon men who had tippled and wenched together in private were attacking each other in public for these very same things.

In determination to end the rule of the Whigs, George III had used the Earl of Bute against William Pitt to form a government which would uphold Royal Prerogative. Wilkes publicly declaimed that Dashwood had been made Chancellor 'because of his skill with tavern bills' and he referred to Bute as 'the damned Scotsman and his government'. Such animosities after friendships which had been so warm were neither forgiven or forgotten.

Dashwood, who had restored the family motto of *Pro Magna Charta*[1] when he became a peer, was appointed Lord Lieutenant of Buckinghamshire in May 1763. He was also commanding officer of the Bucks Militia, with John Wilkes serving under him.

On the fall of the Rockingham Ministry in 1766 Pitt came into his own again. The King was forced to ask him to form a government and this he did, though it was an unstable

1. It is spelt thus. The motto was adopted by the Dashwood family shortly after the r ebellion of 1688, to which it refers.

coalition. Lord le Despencer (as Dashwood now was) was surprisingly appointed Postmaster-General, an administrative rather than a political post in those days. But this did not deter the Duke of Newcastle from regarding the appointment as proof that Pitt was openly seeking an alliance with Bute, and North alleged that this was part of Pitt's plan to strengthen the Government in the House of Lords.

Yet as Postmaster-General, le Despencer was as great a success as he was a failure at the Exchequer. He took his work seriously, being an efficient administrator and initiating many beneficial changes. He retained the post until his death in December 1781. As Postmaster-General he frequently clashed with M.P.s who regarded the appointment of local deputy postmasters as part of the patronage privileges to which their membership of Parliament entitled them. He was responsible for co-ordinating the Inland Post, Foreign Letter Post, Penny Post and Cross Roads Letter Post. In the course of his duties he became closely acquainted with the American Postmaster-General, Benjamin Franklin, who was a frequent visitor to West Wycombe.

This friendship with Franklin, who from 1764 to 1775 was in Britain to represent the views of the American colonies against direct taxation of America by the British Parliament, was another indication of le Despencer's appreciation of men of talent regardless of their political affiliations. Together these two men discussed the problems of the two continents and the need for a greater understanding between them. Dashwood was more far-sighted than his colleagues in realizing the need for Anglo-American co-operation and a greater spirit of give-and-take on this side of the Atlantic. And out of this association came a surprising co-operative effort, when one bears in mind le Despencer's reputed scorn for organized religion. In 1773 the two men produced a revised Book of Common Prayer for the Church of England, the purpose of which was a humanitarian one – 'to prevent the old and faithful from freezing to death through long ceremonies in cold churches, to make the services so short as to attract the young and lively, and relieve the well-disposed from the inflection of interminable prayers'. This was le Despencer's personal version of their aims, and its breezy, reforming zest surely disposes of the argument that le Despencer was playing the humbug when he undertook this work.

In fact, Dashwood was already working on the Liturgy before Franklin arrived in Britain. He had reduced the Catechism to two sensible and practical questions: (1) what is your duty to God; and (2) what is your duty to your neighbour?

According to one source le Despencer had the Revised Prayer Book printed in Wycombe at his own expense in 1773, but the copy in the British Museum contains the imprint of a printer in St. Paul's Churchyard. The Franklin-Despencer Prayer Book was ignored by the British Bishops, so the authors decided to make it the basis for future services of the Church in America. And so it remains to this day, the Americans showing more eagerness for reform than the tradition-bound Bishops in Britain.

Franklin considered le Despencer to be not only the man more than any other who 'has re-organized the postal services of England and provided something like a national postal service', but 'a humane, liberal reformer in Church affairs'. He also refers to his friend making 'a handsome contribution to the Unitarian Chapels' – an act of almost extreme religious tolerance and charity on the part of a member of the Church of England in the eighteenth century.

These views are of the utmost importance in arriving at a true assessment of the character of the Squire of West Wycombe. Franklin, one of the ablest men of his age, was a keen judge of character and it is unthinkable that in a long association with le Despencer he was deceived by him.

What was this strange man's true character? On the credit side are many virtues, honesty, love of the classics, patron of the arts, competent administrator and, according to John Wilkes, 'a first-class commanding officer of the Militia'. On the debit side are many less pleasant features, but it is hard to say where truth ends and legend begins. It is probably right to assert that he was not nearly as licentious and dissolute as he was painted and that he was the victim of political mischief-makers who did not hesitate to blacken his character to further their own ends.

There are few examples of his political courage and strong sense of injustice so typical as that of his advocacy of fair play for Admiral Byng. In 1756 Byng fought an unsatisfactory action off Minorca and was accused of not engaging the enemy more closely. At the subsequent court-martial he was convicted of not having done his best and sentenced to be shot. Dashwood – as he then was – campaigned vigorously both in and out of Parliament for Admiral Byng, arguing on the grounds of 'common humanity and decency' that the Admiral was being treated barbarically. In doing this he might easily have jeopardized his whole political future, for he challenged the highest powers in the land and clashed with the powerful Duke of Newcastle. But these efforts did not save Byng, who was executed at Portsmouth in 1757.

In relating the full story of the Brotherhood of 'Saint' Francis in ensuing chapters, a clearer picture of his activities in founding that mysterious society will emerge. But before telling this story it is necessary to examine the puzzle of le Despencer's religious convictions. This is not such an academic poser as it sounds, for the mystery of the club is bound up with it. How could a man noted for his antipathy to religion blandly assume the patronage of his local church and spend long hours with Benjamin Franklin revising the Prayer Book? Was this just an example of the man's hypocrisy, or is it possible that somewhere the facts have been mixed up?

Francis was too honest and forthright a man to descend to such blatant and indeed unnecessary hypocrisy. Nothing in his character suggests that he would do so. It should also be remembered that, even if he practised deception on Franklin, the latter would certainly have heard of the rumours of the Brotherhood's satanic rites. He could not have failed to hear them.

It has been suggested that in his old age le Despencer reformed and that his efforts in revising the Prayer Book and his rebuilding of West Wycombe Church were attempts to

45

make amends for past follies and vices. This suggestion is feasible, but again on the available evidence it is in no way conclusive. It is almost certain that he continued his weird practices in the caves long after the church was rebuilt and after he was supposed to have reformed. And there is the testimony of John Wilkes that the glistening golden ball on top of St. Lawrence's Church at West Wycombe was 'the best Globe Tavern I was ever in', which indicates that members of the Brotherhood met there. Wilkes referred to drinking 'divine milk punch' inside the ball with le Despencer and Churchill.

A clue to Francis's outlook on religion is to be found in various incidents in his young manhood. Describing an episode which took place at Rome during Holy Week, Walpole told how Dashwood disguised himself as a night watchman and crept into the Sistine Chapel while the special scourging ceremonies were going on. When the lights were put out and the penitents commenced to flagellate themselves in a manner so gentle that it hardly appeared like atonement, Francis drew a horse whip out from under his cloak and strode up and down the aisle, lashing out at all who were near him. The chapel rang to agonized and hysterical shrieks of *El Diavolo!*

There are several versions of this incident. One suggests that it was a youthful prank by one who had a great contempt for Romish practices. Yet another says that Dashwood was shocked that the penitents should fail to lash themselves with such little force and that, in a mood of self-righteousness and piety, he decided to teach them a lesson and administer his own punishment. But the more accurate judgement would seem to be that of Louis C. Jones in *Clubs of the Georgian Rakes,* who spoke of Dashwood as 'a madcap prankster fascinated by a religion in which he could not believe'.

If art, combined with a love of Latin, was his most serious study in his youth, occultism became an absorbing hobby. Francis's first recorded interest in black magic was on a visit to France, when he attended a black mass as a curious but not particularly impressed spectator. But in Italy, where the occult was extensively practised in Venice and the south, casual interest turned into a passion for collecting data and hieroglyphics of the mumbo-jumbo of satanism. His chroniclers point out that this is evidence of the instability of his temperament and suggest he suffered from a Poesque mania for the bizarre. Undoubtedly he was attracted to the fantastic in both its erotic and demoniac manifestations, but, so, too, have been other famous and respected men. There is really very little proof that either in his early life or in the heyday of his rakism that he did more than play with black magic as an idea. He was not as superstitious as has been alleged; indeed, throughout his life he displayed a healthy scepticism of things which could not be logically explained. This is even more remarkable when one recalls that the eighteenth century was still an age of superstition, when devils and the supernatural were accepted as realities by educated people. Even John Wesley had a personal as well as a religious belief in devils. The Dashwood attitude was to mock at these things, and it was through this mockery that he acquired his reputation as a black magician.

His passion for black magic was in part at least a reaction against Papism, for which early on in life he developed a deep and ineradicable hatred. Perhaps his tutor was to blame. This seriously minded but unsuitable companion for a young blood tried hard to convert Francis to the Catholic Church. The more he tried the more his pupil scoffed and ridiculed. The Rev. Arthur Plaisted, author of *The Manor and Parish Records of Medmenham*, who might be expected to be among the severest critics of Francis, showed more sympathy than others when he wrote: 'in his youth Francis Dashwood had been thoroughly disgusted at the superstitious monastic proceedings to which he had constantly been taken by a well-meaning but unwise tutor'.

As has been mentioned there were Jacobite sympathizers in his family, and they probably wished to find a tutor who would share their views. Charles Johnston makes reference to this in *Chrysal*: 'The religious principles established in the country whither he was sent for education and the political ones it was designed he should assist to establish at home were so intimately connected that it was impossible to find a tutor for him sufficiently attached to his family not secretly inclined to Rome.' Johnston tries to make out that Francis was superstitious and tells a story about his being so scared one night by the appearance of a cat on his bed that he ran to his tutor and promised to reform and attend religious services and never again to mock. Johnston, a writer who sadly lacked clarity, gave the impression than Francis was always secretly in fear of the supernatural powers in religion. But Johnston's information was not merely second-hand, but frequently third-hand and from not very reliable sources in all cases.

Francis was essentially independent-minded and neither his tutor nor his family influenced him in the least. We have seen how he eschewed Jacobitism and a detestation of Papism led – perhaps through the influence of Voltaire – to an active dislike of all forms of religion in his early days. Yet this did not prevent him from fulfilling his duties as a supporter of the Church of England, for, as Squire of West Wycombe the living of the Church of St. Lawrence was in his patronage.

True, he was a patron who often behaved in a puzzling manner, lending some credence to the theory that he may have been quietly mocking the Church while contributing to its funds. Churchill wrote of St. Lawrence's Church after Dashwood had rebuilt it:

> 'A temple built aloft in air
> That serves for show and not for prayer.'

In this lies another clue to the puzzle of Francis's character. He was an inveterate showman. He could not resist showmanship, and just as his love of black magic, mysterious caves and midnight orgies reflects this tendency, so, too, does his work in rebuilding the church. He could not resist creating something that would cause a stir and attract controversy.

He had a deep-rooted hatred for cant and humbug in religion. From an educational standard he was far better equipped mentally than the average parson of his day. Most of the eighteenth-century parsons were semi-literate and, what was worse, a dissolute crowd of hard-drinking, hard-swearing reprobates who spent most of their time hunting. Few of them led exemplary lives, many combined fornication and preaching. Many of them were responsible for the scandal of the Fleet marriages which culminated in Lord Hardwicke's Bill in 1753, requiring banns to be called on three successive Sundays before marriage, and at the same time prohibiting the publication of banns if parents objected to the match. Many rascally clergymen went round touting for marriages, and the Fleet marriages ramp was, as Charles Knight tells in his *London*, first thought up by a group of disreputable clergymen imprisoned for debt in the Fleet Jail. But not until the fashion of Fleet marriages infiltrated into society was there any move to suppress them.

Francis had little time for the clergy and openly despised many of them. His instinct was to revolt against the religion of the day and he certainly preferred Voltaire to the Bible. But, like Voltaire, he was liberal and tolerant and never carried his antagonism to the point of being positively atheistic. Probably he accepted his position as patron of the Church of St. Lawrence as part of his public duties, and, as such, buried his prejudices and tried to carry them out. But he never did this in a hypocritical manner and could never resist a sly dig at ecclesiastical pomposity.

On 3 July, 1763, the Church of St. Lawrence was re-opened and, it is recorded, 'the chimes of the bells rang out to pay tribute to the pious generosity of Lord le Despencer'. The new organ alone had cost him £6,000.

Immediate reaction to the church was one of bewilderment and embarrassment on the part of the parishioners, bewilderment because they were not sure whether they were meant to admire this as a work of art, or whether it was a colossal joke in the worst possible taste.

Perhaps Francis wanted to make sure that whatever he created would always be remembered, but it also seems likely that he took on impish delight in debunking the solemnity of the traditional church and, at the same time, determined that it should convey something of his impatience with old-fashioned religious conventions. In its extravaganzas and impish touches the new building was a revolt against Papist ideas, but in putting in an organ and providing unusual embellishments it was equally a revolt against Puritanism. There is no denying that the new church was revolutionary in design. Perhaps he thought a church with a bizarre golden ball perched on its summit would improve the view from West Wycombe House.

The tower of St. Lawrence is eighty feet high up and the golden ball which tops it is another twenty. Inside the ball there is ample space for a small gathering. Wilkes, with his inimitable talent for satire, wrote of the church: 'Some churches have been built for devotion, others from parade of vanity. I believe this is the first church which has ever been built for a prospect . . . built on the *top* of a hill for the convenience and devotion of the town at the *bottom* of it. . . . I admire the silence and secrecy which reigns in that great globe, undisturbed, but by his jolly songs very unfit for the profane ears of the world below.'

This is a reference to occasions on which Wilkes and Churchill had tippled with Dashwood in the golden ball. If these statements of Wilkes are correct, then the friendship of the three men must have been maintained after the political dissensions which largely broke up the Brotherhood. This is another of the unsolved puzzles of the period, for, if this trio were drinking and singing together in such incongruous surroundings, it is certain that at the same time Wilkes and Churchill were writing uncomplimentary tracts and verses about their host and lampooning his private life.

There can be no conclusive verdict on Francis's religious beliefs or disbeliefs, but they cannot be said to be more unorthodox than, say, the present Dean of Canterbury. The fact that Dr. Hewlett Johnson was a bigoted supporter of atheist Russia and its communist creed did not prevent his carrying out his duties in the Church of England faithfully. Nor, apparently, did Francis's antipathy to organized religion and his hobby of black magic prevent his being a generous patron of his Church. Whatever the arguments may be, there is no denying that he had less than justice done to him in the churlish acknowledgements of his revision of the Prayer Book. Historians have given almost all the credit for this to Franklin, yet it was Francis who took the initiative in this work and asked Franklin to assist him. The book, which was published for private circulation in 1773, was entitled *The Franklin Prayer Book,* but there is some foundation for the story that the original version, which bore le Despencer's name on the title page, was suppressed by the Church authorities in Britain. The work was studiously ignored in this country.

One can well imagine that Francis's love of things beautiful, his delight in intelligent conversation, his wit and fondness for Latin tags and sonnets he composed in this language, would endear him to Franklin. His interest in the arts extended from architecture to painting, of which he was a connoisseur as well as a generous patron, from poetry to the theatre and literature. In 1756 he presented a copy of Pliny's Epistles to the Bodleian Library at Oxford.

Francis's last days were spent quietly entertaining his friends at West Wycombe, where, after his wife's death, he lived with a former actress, a Mrs. Barry, 'an agreeable woman, lively and easy to live with', he described her. After his death Herbert Croft, who had known him well, paid this two-edged tribute:

'. . . the most careless and perhaps the most facetious libertine of his age. . . . His notions were peculiar to himself and originated from a species of good humour, highly commendable, though it has not obtained, universally, with the less eccentric part of mankind.'

So the enigma of his character remains with us, baffling, mysterious and fascinating. It is ironical that he is remembered for none of the things mentioned in this chapter, neither for his political career, his patronage of the arts nor his revision of the Prayer Book, but for the part he played in giving rise to the legend of the Hell-Fire Club. And thus from documentary narrative one must turn into a tangled path of fact and fiction, of positive clues and lurid legend in quest of the more exciting, if less edifying, story of one of the strangest clubs which ever existed.

CHAPTER 3

AT THE SIGN OF THE VULTURE

UNDER the flickering lamplight at a corner of St. Michael's Alley, in Cornhill, London, one winter's evening in 1746, a sparsely-clad girl, pale, pinched and sad, with wistful eyes, might have been seen alone and shivering.

Nor was it entirely due to the chill, damp night air that she drew her scanty apparel closer round her thin little body. A short distance away, swinging slowly in the wind, and creaking malevolently as it did so, was an inn sign forbidding enough to induce anyone to shiver. As the sign swung to and fro the lamplight illuminated the hooked beak of a hideous and repulsive vulture, poised ready to swoop.

It was the sign of the George and Vulture.

One may see this inn today, though not since 1860 has it been used for residential purposes. There is nothing particularly sinister about its appearance now, and indoors at least it has a cosy, Pickwickian atmosphere. And, indeed, there is good reason for this, as a small figure of the redoubtable Mr. Pickwick, carved in wood, greets one, and on the walls are the familiar illustrations from Dickens's novels. For it was here that Mr. Pickwick settled himself when he escaped from the clutches of the crafty Mrs. Bardell.

The George and Vulture dates back long before Dickensian times. Stow, pin-pointing its site exactly, described it as existing under the sign of the George in 1598. But sometime in the mid-eighteenth century the landlord of the George, a man of unaccountable tastes, went to Peckham Fair, and seeing there exhibited a rare bird catalogued as 'a most noble and extraordinary cock vulture', bought it. For a long period he kept the vulture in his inn yard, at the same time adding the title of 'Vulture' to that of the George.

Goldsmith, who had a nose for the sinister and kept a

notebook of anything phenomenal that he saw or heard, swore that the George and Vulture was 'the most uncanny of all inns in London'. He mentioned that it was presided over by a landlord who 'delights in tales of the supernatural and once kept a cock vulture with which he scared his audience with accounts of its alleged supernatural powers'. He also mentioned that the inn was burnt down in 1748 and entirely rebuilt.

On the night in question the landlord, a man whose visage was almost as repulsive as that of the vulture on the inn sign, came to a side door and whistled.

The girl started, drew her cloak down over her head so that her features were hidden and crossed the road towards him.

'You have brought it, m'dear?' he inquired in a sibilant whisper.

'Yes, I have it,' she replied almost inaudibly.

She hesitated, looking around her furtively.

'You need not be afraid. The Old One will not eat you. Wait here, while I tell him you have arrived.'

The landlord passed into a private room. Here, drinking claret which had been mulled slightly over a log fire, sat a prematurely aged man, wearing a red velvet smoking cap, his thin mouth clenched tightly over a long, curling pipe. By his side was a younger, pleasant-faced man with a ruddy countenance and a smile playing around a wide, generous mouth. The two men presented a remarkable contrast in appearance, the aged, rather pretentious intellectual and the rosy-faced country squire with patrician good looks.

The former was Paul Whitehead, paid hack writer of the Tory Party, propagandist of the 'Prince's Friends', of whom Charles Churchill wrote:

'May I (can worse disgrace on manhood fall?)
Be born a Whitehead and baptized a Paul?'

His companion was Sir Francis Dashwood, Member of Parliament for Romney.

'Gentlemen, the messenger has brought the book you wish.'

53

'Then bring her in,' said Whitehead.

The landlord opened the door and motioned the girl to enter. As he did so Whitehead signalled to him to withdraw.

'Come over into the candlelight that I can see you properly,' whispered 'Paul the Aged', 'and don't be frightened.'

'Sir,' replied the girl, 'I must not, I durst not stay. Here is what you desire.'

And she drew from her cloak a book bound in red morocco and placed it on the table by the bottle of claret.

'Stay at least until I have examined it. I may have some questions to put to you.'

He picked up the book and slowly turned over the leaves, nodding as though satisfied, and occasionally his eye lit up and he chuckled. Then, without a word, he passed the volume to Dashwood. The latter looked at it silently but more intensely, holding it up to the light and impatiently flicking through the pages.

'Without a doubt this is it. A copy, of course, but absolutely authentic as far as I can see. The sign of the pentagram and the secrets of the triangle. All is here. And the full Latin verse of the Venetian Black Mass. I compliment you, Paul, on being able to secure something I believed was unobtainable in this country.'

Whitehead's eyes were fixed on the girl. 'And you brought this book from the usurper of good Master Curll's trade?'

'I am to mention no names other than to say it is with Master Coustance's compliments, if it pleases you, sir.'

'And indeed it does so please,' chipped in Dashwood, slapping his palm down on the table and with it two gold sovereigns. 'Give this as recompense to your Master Coustance, if that be his name. I assume he has taken over the business of Master Curll, undoubtedly the most enterprising printer London ever had, rascal though he might have been.'

The girl took the money and tucked it into her dress. For a moment she hesitated.

'But, of course, you are awaiting your own reward as

porter of this precious book. Here –' and he tossed a coin at her.

'It is not for that I am waiting. My master wished me to say, sir, that he doesn't want his name to be mentioned, if it pleases your noble selves. And I – I, sir, I want nothing for my trouble.'

'Nothing!' exclaimed both men in amazement.

'I am superstitious, you see, if you will forgive me. I am afeared of that book and would want no reward for handling it.'

'In the name of good King George, child, what do you mean. Surely you do not read Latin? What do you know of this work?'

'Nothing, except – well, except that I know it is a work of the Devil.'

'And who told you that fine story? Not Master Coustance, I warrant.'

'No, sir. It was Master Goldsmith who said that when he called to see Master Curll one day. Happened as he saw the book while it was being bound and he told Master Curll, "If you let that book into innocent hands you will loose Beelzebub himself in London." That was some years ago, and I have heard Master Coustance tell the story often enough. The book has always stayed locked up in his safe.'

'And are you as innocent as you look, child?' leered Whitehead. 'Have you no personal knowledge of the Devil? Are you so unsullied that you pretend to shrink like a shy violet?'

The girl shook her head. 'I am poor, sirs, but I have no wish to be contaminated, not for all the gold you might offer me.'

'Go then, my child, and do not waste our time with your idle chatter. If you disdain our money, go and console yourself with your virginal charms. I take it you are trying to convince us that you are a maid?'

She did not reply.

'Silence, eh? You are not so bold as to try to tell us more unlikely stories. Ah, well, perhaps if you will not admit that

55

you have no maidenhead, you will have a glass of claret to warm you on your way.'

For a moment the girl looked thoughtful. It was as though she hadn't heard what he had said. Then:

'I apologize if I may seem untruthful, but please do not misunderstand my silence. It is simply that I do not wish you to judge me by the contents of that book.'

Dashwood intervened: 'Paul, you old cynic, you have shocked her just as you shocked Elizabeth Carter[1] and so many other good young women. The poor girl is scared out of her wits. I'll swear she is a virgin even though she may work for the printer of the most obscene books in London. A virgin hawking whoremongering pamphlets, can you match that for superb self-confidence in her ability to defend her maidenhead! They tell me this man, Coustance, has a monopoly of the best printed lists of all the harlots from Whitechapel to Drury Lane.'

He poured out a glass of claret, raised it in her direction and handed it over with a flourish. 'Please accept our apologies. Do not offer your own. You have nothing to apologize for. Drink this glass and I promise it will give you back your speech and drive away any fears of bewitchment. It is you yourself who is bewitching, far more so than the book. I assure you that neither Mr. Whitehead here – a gentle satirist, if I may say so – nor I are black magicians. We do not seek to conjure up the evil spirits, but to indulge in a little wholesome play – to use this book to show what nonsense the world thinks and talks.'

Dashwood was charming and kindly where Whitehead, a fumbler, was merely clumsy and lascivious. His gesture seemed to set the girl at her ease, for she took the glass and sipped from it, slowly and meditatively.

'I thank you, sir, for your pretty speech.'

'And what is your name, child?'

'I am known as Mary.'

'How oddly you reply to questions. You are "known as Mary". But you are very much more than a Mary. With your sad eyes and your slim child's figure, you are much

1. Translator of *Epictetus* and a famous blue-stocking of the period.

more an Agnes. Yes, the spit image of St. Agnes, that Roman virgin who was beheaded at twelve. Eh, Whitehead?'

'For one who claims to be a maid doubtless it is a charming name, providing it doesn't mean she must live up to it. But tell me, do you never look at these books you deliver to clients?' said Paul.

'Never. Master Coustance knows that.'

'But I warrant you know the contents of many of them?'

'I know, gentleman, that they are not for the eyes of one as young as I.'

'And how young are you?'

'Twelve this year, and it pleases you.'

'You look older, child.'

'I swear that is my true age.'

'Twelve,' cried Dashwood triumphantly. 'I knew it. The very age at which St. Agnes died.'

'You show sound common sense for your age,' intervened Whitehead again. 'How would you like a new master?'

'Master Coustance has been very good. He gives me shelter.'

'That does not answer my question. Master Coustance, I warrant, doesn't give you enough money to dress warmly these chill winter nights. You could do with a warmer cloak.'

But whatever ideas may have been hatching in Whitehead's mind were rudely interrupted by a knock at the door. In bustled the landlord, hands spread out deprecatingly.

'Gentlemen, please forgive me. I was in the buttery and I thought the little she-devil had left. I see that she is wasting your time. Come, you must go at once.'

'We are wasting hers, landlord. Or so it would seem. No, no, let her finish her glass of claret. Tell us, landlord, do you know her well?'

'Not I, sir. I cannot speak for her.'

'Well, the child seems uncommonly scared. Perhaps your vulture frightened her. But she is a pretty little wench and she would make a useful acquisition for members of the Divan Club,' observed Whitehead.

'*Not* the Divan Club,' interrupted Dashwood. 'There is

something about her that is unique. She's so strangely poised for one so young. Here is a child who could be moulded into something.'

'You are thinking of Pygmalion, San Francesco?' inquired Paul with a guffaw.

'Pygmalion?' repeated Dashwood. 'Pygmalion. You have given me an idea. Oh, to have been Pygmalion, not just to carve a statue and ask Venus to breathe life into it. But to take a living statue and mould it into one's ideal.'

'You think —'

'Not what you are thinking. I am not clear what I think. The claret has fuddled me. But I see the germ of an idea. Tomorrow it may become positive and take wings.'

'And now, sirs, I must, an you will forgive me, take my leave. And I thank you most graciously for the glass of wine.'

'Tell Master Coustance to let me have his latest guide book tomorrow. He will know what I mean. And bring it here at seven o'clock,' commanded Whitehead.

The girl promised to pass this information on to Master Coustance and made a hurried exit.

'Some more claret, gentlemen?' inquired the landlord.

'Another bottle, please. Now tell me, landlord, have you still got that globe of crystal which used to hang in the parlour?'

'Yes, sir, but it is in the cellar. Some customers objected to it. Said it was a Jacobin relic.'

'The devil they did; You have always scared your customers with your collection of monstrosities,' said Dashwood. 'First your damned vulture, then your three-headed pig, and now your Rosicrucian Lamp. I suppose some of these dam' Whigs thought it was a piece of Jacobite jiggery-pokery, eh? However, do not worry. Leave it in the cellar, but keep it lighted from now on. And in future we will come here to sup and drink in the cellar under that light. For what better place for a new society of wits than your cellar under the Everlasting Light of the Rosicrucians, and knowing that your evil vulture is swinging on the inn sign.

58

How say you, Paul? The sign of the Vulture. A pretty place for something novel in club life. The sign, the lamp and, for good measure and instruction, this book. A damp cellar and moisture dripping from the ceiling.'

'I can attend to that, sir, if you really wish to use the cellar,' said the landlord anxiously.

'Leave it as it is. I would appreciate the change of environment. Such a change from the Dilettanti and the Divan.'

'You have made up your mind, then?' asked Paul.

'Assuredly. But I have another excellent reason for selecting this tavern and its cellar for a select and witty body of companions. You do not deny, landlord, that the George and Vulture was once the headquarters of one of the Hell-Fire clubs?'

The landlord paled.

'Alas, sirs, I had hoped that no one remembered that. It was long ago when the vulture was alive. The clubs, as you know, sir, were closed by proclamation, and we complied with the law. You would not hold that against me, sir?'

'Not as long as you promise to convert your roomy cellar into our new headquarters. And the password for members, landlord, will be just four simple words – *San Francesco di Wycombe*. You will remember that?'

'*San Francesco di Wycombe*. I will try to remember it, sir. And tomorrow I will see that the cellar is prepared for you. And the lamp will be lit.'

In such circumstances did the Brotherhood of 'Saint' Francis come to be formed under the foreboding sign of the Vulture.

This much it is possible to reconstruct. Doubtless the landlord was afraid for his reputation when Dashwood reminded him that one of the original Hell-Fire clubs had its headquarters there. For the edict banning these clubs had caused great consternation among many tavern keepers. Lord Macclesfield, Lord High Chancellor, had initiated a King's Order in Council for 'calling together the

Justices of the Peace for suppressing those blasphemous clubs which are now kept in the Cities of London and Westminster and the suburbs adjacent'.

'One of these infernal meetings,' states a tract of the day, 'is impiously called the Hell-Fire Club, a name very suitable to their diabolical manners.'

The fact that one of the original Hell-Fire clubs had its headquarters at the George and Vulture is in part responsible for the origins of the Brotherhood of 'Saint' Francis being so obscure. When, many years ago, it was suggested that the Brotherhood was founded at the George and Vulture, this was emphatically refuted on the grounds that the Dashwood fraternity had been confused with the earlier Hell-Fire Club. Various estimates have been made of the probable date when the Brotherhood was founded. Some have asserted that it started in 1742 shortly after Francis Dashwood returned from his second visit to Italy. The Rev. A. H. Plaisted says the evidence 'suggests about 1755', a view shared by Ronald Fuller. This latter date is almost certainly correct in as much as it refers to the club's headquarters at Medmenham Abbey, but there are several references to its existence long before this year. Gordon Maxwell, a reliable authority on old London clubs, confirms that, in its early days, when members of the club were in London, they met at the George and Vulture.

The estimate of 1742, however, seems wide of the mark. Both Whitehead and George Bubb Dodington testified that the 'Knights of Saint Francis' met at the George and Vulture in 1746. There is no earlier mention or record of the society. Dashwood certainly provided the idea for such an institution and the date on which he mooted this must have been either early or late in 1746 – certainly during a winter month when Dashwood was invariably in London. Only Beresford Chancellor in his *Lives of the Rakes* positively gives 1742 as the date of origin and it seems probable that he confused the Brotherhood with either the Dilettanti or the Divan Club, both of which were then flourishing.

Dashwood certainly patronized Edmund Curll, the 'unspeakable Curll', as Ralph Straus called him. This notorious bookseller and printer was an unctuous humbug who, though he traded in Covent Garden under the sign of the Bible, stood in the pillory at Charing Cross in 1725 for 'printing and publishing several obscene and immodest books, greatly tending to the corruption and depravation of manners'. Books for Edmund Curll were printed at the Pope's Head in Rose Street, Covent Garden, and long after his death a surreptitious trade in obscene literature was carried on under his pseudonym by another rogue who maintained this illicit business for private customers only. Dashwood's large pornographic library at West Wycombe contained many of Curll's original works as well as those of his successor who was also a purveyor of black magic treatises, a very limited number of which he had printed for private circulation.

This rogue, whose name was Coustance, was often mentioned by Whitehead, who recalled that '*San Francesco* obtained from Coustance the most cryptic and hell-invoking book from which our rites were most efficaciously *parodied*.' The source for this quotation is Edward Thompson, not perhaps always a reliable witness, but the remark has an authentic ring about it, and Whitehead was the member who kept the Minute Book of the Brotherhood. It is important to note that word '*parodied*'. Here again is a suggestion – perhaps on the merest hint – that the Brothers played at rather than practised black magic. They were adapters rather than adopters, and an example of their fondness for parody can be seen in Whitehead's favourite jest, his celebrated 'poetic epistle of Paul to the Mednamites'.

The reference to the Everlasting Rosicrucian Lamp is of some slight historical and political interest. This lamp was probably one of the many grotesque curios which the landlord of the George and Vulture made a hobby of collecting. An eighteenth-century guide to London describes it as 'a large globe of crystal, encircled by a serpent of pure gold, with its tail in its mouth – a symbol of eternity – and suspended beneath the lamp are chains of twisted snakes; crowning the globe is a pair of silver doves' wings. Set into the ceiling of the cellar of the George and Vulture it signifies the secret badge of a strange Italian society that occasionally meets there.' This 'strange Italian society' must refer to the Franciscans.

The lamp was possibly only loaned to Dashwood when he founded the club, and it was certainly not taken to Medmenham or the caves at West Wycombe, though in the latter a similar lamp was used. But what is significant is the similarity between this Rosicrucian Lamp and the design on the font which Francis Dashwood presented to West Wycombe Church. Round the slender mahogany pillar of the font a serpent is pursuing a dove which is trying to join four others round the bowl at the top. The serpent is ready to strike, but whether this is meant to represent the wisdom of the serpent and the innocence of the doves, or whether the serpent with its head raised ready to strike is symbolical of Satan one cannot tell. It is just another of Francis's puzzling fantasies. But it raises the question whether there was a link between the lamp and the font, whether, in fact, the font was to be a secret reminder to Brothers of their original emblem.

Dashwood's love of the mystical had led him to make a study of Rosicrucianism, which throughout the ages has been the subject of strange controversies. In the eighteenth century some Whigs pretended to find links between the Rosicrucians and the Jacobites, while in our own century Himmler insisted that they were an adjunct of the British Secret Service, according to Mr. H. R. Trevor-Roper! But an examination of the history of the Rosicrucians throws interesting light on Dashwood's mentality. It was in the sixteenth century that tracts began to appear, purporting to reveal the teachings of a secret society founded by Rosencreutz, and magical and hypnotic powers were claimed by practitioners of this movement. Some years later a report gained currency to the effect that the author of one of these tracts was a pious Stuttgart pastor named Johann Valentine Andreae, who had written it to ridicule the cult for secret doctrines then fashionable among the learned. It may well be that Dashwood, knowing this, borrowed some of the symbols of Rosicrucianism to indulge in his favourite pastime of burlesquing superstitious beliefs.

Equally is it feasible that he heard of Rosicrucianism in Jacobite circles in Rome. If this is so, the choice of a Rosicrucian lamp for the club's emblem, with its Jacobite association, may have been a counterblast against the formation in this same year – 1746 – of a club to celebrate the Battle of Culloden with an annual banquet on 16 April. In the *Gentleman's Magazine* there appeared the following advertisement:

'Half-Moon Tavern, Cheapside, 13 April. His Royal Highness the Duke of Cumberland having restored peace to Britain by the ever-memorable Battle of Culloden, fought on the 16th of April, 1745, the *choice spirits* have agreed to celebrate that day annually by a Grand Jubilee in the Moon, of which the Stars are hereby acquainted and summoned to shine with their brightest Lustre by six o'clock on Thursday next in the Evening.'

Playboy, rake, seducer, wine-bibber and masquerader as he was, Dashwood at no time completely lost touch with reality. He was an escapist not from life and duty, but from the mundane and the humdrum. This trait in his character has been missed by his chroniclers. Had he wished to escape from life and duty, nothing would have been easier for him than to spend the rest of his days in his beloved Italy. But he used clubs not only for companionship, but as a medium for his escapist philosophy and gave full rein to his imaginative flights in planning large-scale fantasies. Certainly he dabbled in black-magic, but always, as far as one can gather, in a light-hearted, make-believe manner, and nearly always it was to propagate his pet theme that superstition was the opiate of the people. He was, in fact, an aristocratic Marxist in his radical, implacable hatred of Popery, Anglican 'white magic'[1] as he once termed the enthusiasm of a High Churchman's fondness for ritual, evangelistic emotionalism and any other deviations from matter-of-fact, down-to-earth Protestantism. He lost no opportunity of ridiculing such

1. Letter to George Selwyn.

excesses, as he considered them to be, and used his influence as head of the Brotherhood to instil into its members the need for steering clear of such perversions of true religion.

The suggestion has even been made that the Brotherhood was 'founded in a zeal for Protestantism'. One finds this view a little hard to swallow, but it would be true to say that its members had a common detestation of Catholicism and that its activities were in part a parody of Romish practices. Charles Johnston summed it up as 'a society in burlesque imitation of religious societies which are instituted in other countries'. John Wilkes in one volume of *The New Foundling Hospital for Wits* said that the Brotherhood 'among other amusements sometimes have mock celebrations of the more ridiculous rites of the foreign religious orders among Roman Catholics and Franciscans in particular'. The anonymous author of *Nocturnal Revels*, who described himself as 'A Monk of the Order of Saint Francis', told how Dashwood disapproved of foreign 'religious seminaries founded in direct contradiction of Nature and Reason', and that he determined on returning to England to deflate such pretensions by means of a burlesque society which would mock their rites and not enforce celibacy on members.

The Rev. Arthur Plaisted referred to the Order of 'Saint' Francis as 'a society of dabblers in art and literature', which is a very different proposition. This statement cannot be dismissed as the ignorance of a cleric innocent of any knowledge of the club's legends. For he went on to claim that the society was later 'lampooned as the Hell-Fire Club' and lent credence to the theory that the most preposterous allegations about the Brotherhood were malicious political propaganda by enemies of Dashwood.

Elizabeth Montagu declared that: 'Francis Dashwood is a man most unique in his religious foresight. His Bishop is pleased to inform me that he has a passion for ecclesiastical reform which might appear alarmingly radical were he not also a gentleman and a Tory. "Sir Francis is a bulwark of the Church, yet he dissents in order to give assent to his foremost convictions. He would not hesitate to summon Bell, Book and Candle, if he had any premonition that some person desired to introduce superstitious or Popish practices in our midst."'

Thus it is more than likely that in its early stages the Brotherhood of 'Saint' Francis was more a playful burlesque than a serious attempt at creating a new club. The fact that there are no records of these early days of the society appears to confirm this. Possibly Francis was bored with the Divan and the Dilettanti, or perhaps he delighted in the macabre curiosities of the George and Vulture, which must have been to mid-eighteenth century London what Dirty Dick's was to the nineteenth and Charlie Brown's Limehouse tavern became in the twentieth. Had this inn not been burned down in 1748, it might have been equally as famous as that of the celebrated Charlie.

Mention has already been made of the painting of Francis, decked out in monastic robes and suitably tonsured as he pored diligently over a miniature statue of Venus. Knapton, who was commissioned to make portraits of all members of the Dilettanti (any member who failed to have such a portrait executed was fined), may even have created in Dashwood's mind the idea for such a club. One does not know for certain whether the Brotherhood existed before Knapton made this painting, or if this was merely Knapton's own conception of Dashwood. It may have been something he thought up himself, for he painted each member in abnormal guise – Sandwich for example, as a Turk. What is certain is that this painting attracted more attention and doubtless more guffaws and witticisms than that of any other member, and it could have been that Knapton was himself the creator of 'Saint' Francis when he added a halo to his subject's head.

The fire at the George and Vulture must have ended the associations of the Brotherhood with this inn. There is no proof that further meetings were held when the inn was rebuilt.

From 1748 until about 1755 there are discrepancies in available evidence about the club's existence. This is possibly due to the informality of the gatherings at the George and Vulture which were probably shared by not more than three or four men – most likely Dashwood, Whitehead, Dodington and Sandwich. Some add the name of Joseph (Giuseppe) Mattia Borgnis to those of founder-members of the club, but as Sir Francis did not bring this painter over to England from his native Craveggio in Italy until 1751, this seems unlikely. It is almost certain that there were no formal minutes of the gatherings at the George and Vulture, which is one reason why the earliest mention of the society in its original documents was dated 1750. Unfortunately most of the papers relating to the club, and including Paul Whitehead's Minute Book, have been destroyed. Even the evidence about who destroyed them is confusing. Paul Whitehead's biographer, Captain (later Commodore) Edward Thompson, said that Whitehead burnt a large quantity of his papers during the three days before his death, a statement which was confirmed by Thomas Langley, who assumed that these included the Minute Book. The present Mr. Francis Dashwood, however, states that 'The Minute Book is supposed to have been destroyed by Lord Sandwich. Many other papers were destroyed in a bonfire at West Wycombe Park about eighty years ago.'

But if the society met in 1750, where was their meeting place? Not at the George and Vulture, and, as the Rev. Arthur Plaisted pointed out, it is most unlikely that they had Medmenham Abbey as their headquarters then, for the correspondence of Francis Duffield, who made the abbey into a three-storey dwelling, shows that he was still living there at the time. And in 1750 the caves were not created. Plaisted's claim that the society was founded about 1755, however, as we have seen, is inaccurate in so far as the George and Vulture records go. And, as such members as Dodington and Whitehead mention the Franciscans in 1752 and 1753, it rules out the possibility that the club suspended its activities from 1748 until 1755.

The only possible clues to what went on in this period we will examine in detail in the next chapter.

Meanwhile there remains the riddle of the unusual girl messenger who brought the handbook on the occult to Dashwood and Whitehead at the George and Vulture. Far from being a pallid chit of a girl who appears to have wandered on to this melodramatic stage of the Franciscans by accident, she seems to have quickly established herself as at least an accessory of the society. Indeed, Mary – or Agnes, as Dashwood insisted on calling her – is the missing link in the tale of the Franciscans and, if not the heroine of this story, certainly a recurring and often baffling figure in it.

According to Whitehead she was 'Saint' Agnes. . . .

> 'Demure and ghostly in her silken pall
> Saint Agnes, trembling, glides across the hall.'

This is but an obscure fragment of Whitehead's works, but it can hardly be said to relate to the original saint of that name, more especially as it is followed by a sly reference to 'Charles the preacher, stalking in her wake.' By 'Charles' Whitehead could only have meant Churchill. Thompson, Whitehead's biographer, made no mention of 'Saint Agnes', but Charles Churchill, his *bête noire*, told Robert Lloyd, 'She is the most fascinating and at the same time most mysterious of them all down at Medmenham. I understand she was once an emissary for Coustance in Covent Garden and that it was she who procured Dashwood's infamous books on the Black Arts.'

But for the moment her story must wait.

CHAPTER 4

'DISCIPLES OF BACCHUS AND VENUS'

As it developed and gradually acquired more resplendent headquarters so the title of the club was revised and made more grandiloquent. The 'Brotherhood' was converted into the *Order* of 'Saint' Francis of Wycombe, and later became known as the *Knights* of 'Saint' Francis.

That these escapist romantics were 'a set of worthy fellows, happy disciples of Bacchus and Venus' was the view of Edward Thompson. Captain Thompson was Whitehead's biographer and he probably wished to put the best possible construction on their motives. He wrote of them. 'They occasionally got together to celebrate Woman in wine, and, to give more zest to the festive meeting, they plucked every luxurious idea from the ancients and enriched their own modern pleasures with the addition of classical luxury.'

But how did it all develop? How did a simple little gathering of not more than three or four men grow into a society with a considerable membership, including some of the most distinguished men of the day in art, literature, politics and learning? There is first of all the problem of those 'missing years' from 1748 to 1755.

A slight clue is provided by Mlle Yvette Perrault, of Paris, a descendant of 'Saint Agnes'. Mlle Perrault claims that 'Agnes' married an ancestor of hers, one Léon Perrault, an associate of the Chevalier d'Eon. And, according to the story of 'Saint Agnes', handed down through the generations, Agnes said that after the fire at the George and Vulture there were meetings at Twickenham and 'on an island between Twickenham and Hampton' before the society moved to Medmenham.

Perhaps George Bubb Dodington could enlighten us here, but in the published records of his diary he has omitted to do so. For he lived at Twickenham at this time. Dodington's diary from March 1748 to February 1761 contains many references to Dashwood, but no mention of the Brotherhood is made in the published extracts from the diary. Dodington, however, made it clear in his will that only such extracts as would show him in the best possible light should be made public. An unctuous, rather squalid, podgy humbug, a very different character from Dashwood, he would certainly have wished any references to the club to be deleted.

It may be that somewhere in Twickenham, then, a coterie of literary men, members of the club met to wine and dine and possibly to discuss literary topics. The present Mr. Francis Dashwood says the club is 'supposed to have been formed as an offspring of the Dilettanti Society, a more serious body which Sir Francis had been largely instrumental in forming, and which still plays a valuable part in promoting art in England'.

There is no reason to doubt that literary topics were debated by members and that verses – gracefully constructed, if Rabelaisian in theme – were composed at their gatherings. The original idea was to have a club that was more bohemian than the Dilettanti, one in which arid and sterile intellectualism could be eliminated in favour of a more bacchanalian and earthy flavour.

Search for the island in the Thames 'between Twickenham and Hampton' is not particularly rewarding. It could have been any one of a number of tiny islands along this stretch of the Thames, but there is nothing in the history of any of them which links up with the Brotherhood. One is tempted to believe that Agnes Perrault had little knowledge of the Thames beyond Twickenham and that she was talking vaguely. After all, the distance between Twickenham and Hampton is not inconsiderable, and she cannot have been very sure of her facts to place it so indefinitely. The author of *Nocturnal Revels* wrote of Sir Francis Dashwood having constructed 'a small but elegant building upon a little island in the River Thames not far from Hampton'. This could not have been Medmenham Abbey, and the reference to Hampton to some extent corroborates Agnes Perrault's testimony. One cannot be sure that this author really was, as he claimed, a 'monk of the Order of Saint Francis'. If he were, it is unlikely that so observant and knowledgeable a character would have mistaken Hampton for Medmenham, which is at least twenty miles away.

Charles Johnston, another authority on the Franciscans has been criticized for confusing Medmenham Abbey, West Wycombe House and a temple that existed on an island in the lake of West Wycombe Park, for he wrote:

'A person of flighty imagination and who possessed a fortune that enabled him to pursue that flight, cloyed with common pleasures, and ambitious of distinguishing himself among his companions, to resolve to try if he could not strike out something new, that should at the same time please his own taste and do honour to his genius. The mere gratifications of sense, in their utmost extent, not answering his design, he had recourse to the assistance of imagination to enhance them. . . . In the middle of a large lake upon his estate was an island . . . on this island he erected a building exactly on the model of the monasteries which he had seen in other countries.'

If by this Johnston was indicating Medmenham Abbey, then his statements are quite inaccurate. Dashwood did not build the Abbey, nor was it situated on an island, but on the banks of the Thames. And he certainly built no 'monastery' on an island in the lake of West Wycombe Park. Either Johnston was misinformed and mixed up his facts, or he was referring to some earlier headquarters of the society. He might have been thinking of one of the temples of West Wycombe Park, one of which, a particular obscene architectural effort, was situated on an island in a lake and later destroyed.

Nevertheless, shadowy as is the evidence of any island headquarters for the society, as set forth by Agnes Perrault, the anonymous author of *Nocturnal Revels* and Charles Johnston, in 1956 there came to light among various documents at West Wycombe House a fragment of paper which adds some weight to all this. On this was a statement to the effect that Round Tar Island in the River Thames, between Cookham and Marlow, was 'relinquished' to Lord le Despencer by 'Edward Sawyer, of Cookham, sub-tenant . . . at the request of my landlord, Sir Thomas Stapleton'. The agreement was dated 8 August, 1776.

So, for some unknown reason, the founder of the Franciscans acquired an island, but whether for the society or some other purpose the agreement does not state. It should be noted that by 1776 the Franciscans had long since passed their most active days. But if Stapleton was the landlord of the island, Round Tar may have been used by the Medmenhamites for many years prior to this date.

A wine book of the society (still in existence), dated on its cover 'Medmenham Abbey, 1769' contains a puzzling picture of what looks like a cottage with a hut beside it situated on an island. Certainly the buildings depicted could not possibly be Medmenham Abbey. It might be that the picture has no significance. There is not any artistic merit about it; the cottage and hut are not even picturesque. Could this have been a sketch of Round Tar Island? The hut could have been a boat house.

What appears to be the solution of this problem of the 'missing years' is that during this period the Brothers had no fixed headquarters, but met at various places,[1] possibly somewhere in Twickenham, where some of them lived, perhaps occasionally as guests of Duffield at Medmenham, most certainly as guests of Dashwood at West Wycombe. An island on the Thames may have been a temporary rendezvous.

It is irritating in the extreme that so many writers who mention the club merely hint at what went on at its conclaves. True, most of what anyone can write is largely conjecture, and, given so picturesque a subject, it is not difficult to allow one's imagination to run riot. But there really isn't the excuse for such pompous prudery, such deliberate obscurity and the tantalizing of the reader by the

1. Eyethorpe, the residence of Lord Chesterfield's brother, Sir William Stanhope, has been mentioned as a pre-Medmenham rendezvous.

Victorian practice of rows of asterisks. One comes across such unqualified statements as 'At Medmenham Abbey their orgies became an amateur celebration of the Black Mass', or 'they indulged in every conceivable form of vice and perversion', or the mention in *Follies and Grottoes* of 'a smaller room for nameless vices'.

Much of this description suggests either the blurb for a pornographic novel, or that the Brotherhood was a cross between Nero's Rome, the court of *Louis le Soleil*, ancient rites of the Aztec Indians, the Sicilian deflowering orgies of Aleister Crowley and the cult of the Marquis de Sade.

It adds up to a gross exaggeration of what really took place. There is no evidence whatsoever that any member of the Brotherhood was a sodomite or a flagellant, or that any form of unnatural vice was practised. The Chevalier d'Eon may have been a mincing quean whose sex was the subject of many inquests, mostly verbal, but one at least amounting to a physical inspection. But it is not absolutely certain that he was a member, and he was regarded by the 'Monks' as a butt for their robust brand of humour. Most of the 'Monks' were, it is true, sensualists and lechers, but only the Earl of Sandwich was positively vicious, and then solely in his insatiable pursuit of women.

John Wilkes spoke of 'the younger monks who seemed at least to have sinned naturally . . . in the garden, the grove, the orchard, the neighbouring woods, which all spoke of their loves and frailties'.

Yet the legend that the Franciscans were unspeakable decadents has been perpetuated by many contemporary writers. Wraxhall said the rites of the Knights of Wycombe were 'of a nature subversive of all decency', while Walpole on the other hand dismissed them as merely 'pagan'.

Perhaps the man responsible for many of these *canards* was Charles Johnston, a native of Ireland, who in the years between 1760 and 1765 produced a series of books, to which he added various volumes, entitled *Chrysal: The Adventures of a Guinea*. This work, which contains some highly coloured anecdotes of the period thinly disguised as fiction, owed its immediate success as a best seller not to the technical skill of its author, but because it was regarded as giving an accurate account of many current scandals. *Chrysal* is marked by a singularly laborious style of writing even for the leisurely eighteenth century, its choice of words and phrases is frequently inapt and inept and, at the best, a lamentably poor imitation of Defoe.

Johnston included in his later volumes of *Chrysal* what was obviously intended to be a report on the activities of the Brotherhood. Though this report contains a good many obvious inaccuracies, it is sufficiently factual to suggest that Johnston had much first-hand, or at least second-hand material to work upon. It is generally accepted that his source of information was the poet, Charles Churchill.

Johnston had Catholic sympathies if he wasn't actually a practising Catholic, and these colour his book. Not unnaturally he was disgusted at the idea of religious burlesques. He wrote of Dashwood's 'flighty imagination', yet he certainly gave wings to his own fantasies. . . . 'There was not a vice that he (Dashwood) had ever heard imputed to the inhabitants (*presumably of 'other countries'*) of them for practising for which he did not make provision. The cellars were stored with the choicest wines, the larders with the delicacies of every climate and the cells were fitted up for all purposes of lasciviousness, for which proper objects were also provided.'

And what, one may ask, were these 'proper objects' – unhappy phrase! – provided presumably for improper purposes? Were these merely the 'indecent paintings' to which Wilkes referred, or some of the suggestive status with which Dashwood loved to surprise people in hidden nooks? Or is it just rank, bad writing, not meaning what it says?

It might be deducted that this is an obscure reference to some form of phallic worship. There are similarly diffuse indications of this in the works of John Hall Stevenson, founder of the Demoniacs Club. Stevenson inherited Skelton Castle in Yorkshire in 1733 and had it renamed Crazy Castle. As a friend of Lawrence Sterne, he became imbued with the idea that he was an eighteenth-century Rabelais, and he produced a large number of 'fables' and verses which were little more than Rabelaisian parodies of the works of other people. He was a friend of Dashwood, who was known to the Demoniacs as 'The Privy Councillor'.

Stevenson's close acquaintance with the activities of the Brotherhood and his knowledge of what went on at its meetings suggest that he may well have been one of them. In his *Crazy Tales*, probably composed for the delectation of the Demoniacs, he referred to the 'Franciscan Makaronies of Medmenham and the brethren of Pall Mall, who make use of a Latin of their own manufacture – Makaroni Latin.' Wilkes, incidentally, was also critical of some of Dashwood's Latin texts.

Stevenson also repeatedly mentioned the *Idolum Tentiginis*, which might have been one of the 'proper objects' to which Johnston alluded. This appears to have been a 'hobby horse' similar to that used by the 'women of Israel as part of a religious custom'; they sat astride an idol with the head of a cock, but with a stupendous *fascinum* where the beak should have been. Upon the base was inscribed in Greek *Saviour of the World*. It is of passing interest that the very same motto, also in Greek, was used by Dashwood on the bases of some of his more blatant examples of phallic statuary.

Charles Johnston's turgid narrative continues: 'Thus far the ridicule, however criminal in itself, may seem to have been designed only against those societies of human institutions, but it was beneath his genius to stop here. Nothing less would satisfy him than to attack the very essentials of the religion established by the laws of the country.'

Yet, despite these attacks upon the founder of the Franciscans, Johnston seems to have been impressed by the unique personality of Francis. He referred to him as 'The Superior . . . you see every eye is expressly fixed upon him in admiration at the vivacity, humour and wit in all he does.' Indeed there are few of Dashwood's bitterest critics who do not occasionally balance up their attacks on him with some qualifying remark, however reluctantly, about his pleasant personality.

It is said that many of the club's documents were destroyed eighty years ago because they were 'too obscene for publication'. This may have been an example of Victorian prudery, and perhaps Victorian families were touchier about the skeletons in their forbears' cupboards. But there are at least three sources which positively refute these arguments of obscenity, of black magic and unspeakable orgies. True, two of these sources are members of the club, but, even allowing for their own sympathetic viewpoint, they deserve attention.

Dr. Benjamin Bates, one of the oldest survivors of the Brotherhood – he died in 1828 at the age of ninety-eight – emphatically declared that these stories were 'scandalous and sarcastic fabrications'.

More enlightening is the author of *Nocturnal Revels*, published in 1779. This book is ostensibly a history of and guide book to the most notorious bordellos of London from about 1730–70. In the eighteenth century it was the custom in polite society to refer to bordellos as 'nunneries' or 'abbeys' and bordello-keepers as 'abbesses', and this would explain both why the author included a survey of the Franciscans in the book and why the female members of this club were known as 'nuns'. The word 'nunnery', applied to bordellos, was first introduced by a Mrs. Goadby when she opened a bagnio in Berwick Street, Soho, after a visit to France in the early part of the century. It would, of course, be typical of Dashwood in his fondness for burlesque of Rome to dress the women in nun's attire.

Commenting on the club's activities, this writer, who must have been extremely well-versed in the stews of London, said: 'The salt of these festivities is generally purely Attic, but no indelicacy or indecency is allowed to be intruded without severe penalty.' This is categorical enough, but the author went on to stress that indelicate remarks in mixed company were frowned upon and that fans were provided to 'prevent the ladies' blushes' and to hide them from any accidental, ill-chosen remarks.

One may be cynically distrustful of these comments, bearing in mind the allegations previously mentioned, but it must be remembered that they were written by one who not only claimed to be a member of the club, but who made no attempt to hide its worship of Venus. In comparison with his revelations of the extremes of eroticism (given in great detail) practised at such establishments as Moll King's, 'Mother' Stanhope's and Charlotte Hayes's 'parlour for the aristocracy', the Medmenhamites sound almost respectable.

Sir Max Pemberton made considerable research into the history of the Franciscans in the early part of the twentieth century, not, however for factual study of the society but for background to a romantic novel which he wove around the exploits of the Medmenhamites. This novel was *Sir Richard Escombe*, which, in addition to its fictional characters, also mentioned Dashwood, Wilkes, Churchill and Whitehead. Though, as a work of fiction, the Pemberton novel cannot be regarded as part of the society's bibliography, a good deal of the reconstruction of what went on in Medmenham is based on fact. And, as Pemberton devoted a great deal of time to his research, it is noteworthy that in spite of his unfavourable portrait of the Franciscans, he made this statement in his preface about allegations of satanism: 'That these were an open mockery of established religious faith does not appear to be true . . . the men were mere jesters, but clever jesters.'

In making this statement Sir Max, a meticulously accurate journalist as well as a novelist, went out of his way to refute the findings of *Chrysal* even at the risk of spoiling his own work of fiction.

The *Chrysal* version of the club's worship of Venus is that 'Each member contributed equally towards the cost . . . All was . . . regulated by the strictest economy; the slaves of their lusts being sent back to the brothels from whence they had been brought and the servants of their luxury discharged at the end of every meeting . . . only an old man and woman looked after the place in their absence.'

Both Walpole and Langley gave the impression that there were no servants at Medmenham except for an aged caretaker, but as the former only visited the Abbey in 1763, when he found it 'a very ruinous and bad house' with very poor accommodation, and the latter was there in 1797, it is fairly safe to assume neither had first-hand knowledge of the club in its heyday.

The allegations of Johnston about the 'companions' of the Brothers will be examined later, for the 'Nuns' are of sufficient interest to deserve a chapter to themselves. Meanwhile, to whet our appetite for a more detailed examination of this worship of Venus, it is worth examining the portrait of the 'Monks'' love life drawn by other writers. Barbara Jones in *Follies and Grottoes* draws a picture of the 'Monks' at the Abbey 'drinking wine poured by naked girls and looking at portraits of the Kings of England, which hung above the long drinking sofas in the Chapter House'. Ronald Fuller describes the 'exhausted Friars' going down 'the moonlit river in a pleasure boat, or sporting with their wenches in the reeds'.

Of the fondness for Bacchus among the members there is ample proof. Firm testimony is provided that they both dined and wined well. The wine books of the club, copies of which are still in existence, reveal such interesting data as the following:

'Account of element of wine expended at the private devotion of every Brother when no Chapter had been held . . .

'Brother John of Aylesbury, 12 January, 1761. One bottle of claret.

'Brother John of Aylesbury, 20 March, 1761. One bottle of port.'

'Brother John of Aylesbury' was the pseudonym for John Wilkes, Member of Parliament for Aylesbury and lieutenant colonel in the Bucks militia.

Claret seems to have been the favourite tipple of the Brothers, but port was an obvious preference with some. On 29 September, 1762, 'Thomas de Greys and John of Henley' consumed four bottles of port, two of claret and one of Lisbon at one sitting.

These 'private devotions', judging by the entries in the

wine books, lasted all the year round. They normally consisted of drinking bouts between two or three members, though on many occasions, members like John Wilkes, either came to drink alone, or, as seems more likely, with female company not mentioned in the books.

Sometimes the details of wine consumption are exact to a fraction. Thus, on 1 October, 1760, 'John of Henley Abbot, Francis of Wycombe, Thomas of London, two bottles of claret, one of port and one and seven-eights of calcavello.'

Wilkes was one of the habitual drinkers at Medmenham and his name appears in the wine lists more often than that of anyone else. On 3 October, 1760, he consumed 'two bottles of claret and one of calcavello' at one 'private devotion'. Possibly the claret was for himself and the calcavello for a nameless 'nun'. The previous month he shared with 'Thomas de Greys Abbot' (believed to be Sir Thomas Stapleton) no fewer than 'six bottles of claret, one bottle of port and one of Lisbon'.

Besides claret, port, Lisbon and calcavello, hock, Tenerif, 'white' and Dorchester beer are listed. Wine and liqueurs were provided everywhere for these devotees of Bacchus, though they were mainly wine-drinkers and seem to have followed the fashion of their class in regarding spirits – especially gin – as essentially for the lower orders. How great are the changes in national drinking habits! Not only was there a vast cellar at Medmenham Abbey and probably a buttery[1] in the caves at West Wycombe, but at the Church of St. Lawrence, which he rebuilt, Dashwood installed wine-bins. It is not clear, however, whether the latter were meant to provide sustenance for Francis and his friends before they climbed the ladder to the Golden Ball, or for the nourishment of pew holders during lengthy sermons. Sir Thomas Stapleton paid glowing tribute to the 'Epicurean and Ambrosial Banquets at Mednam, beneath a vast canopy under which a refectory table glistens with sparkling silver and the crystaline purity of fine glass; the food of a most exquisite kind and in gargantuan proportions,

1. The present buttery in the caves is not original; it was put there during reconstruction by Mr. Francis Dashwood.

carefully prepared at the House and brought down to the Abbey where it is served in absolute perfection of detail.'

Francis left about £6,000 worth of wines in his cellars when he died in 1781, which indicates the extent and range of his collection. Menus of the club were in existence during the last century and a typical one includes such items as:

'*Soupe de Sante; Soupe au bourgeoisie;* carp; pupton of partridge; Cullets *a la* Maine; beef; Huffl of — (here the writing is indecipherable, though it is hardly likely to have been "*chien*" as one scribe suggested); a stewed Lyon; and (finally, in extra large letters) PAIN PERDU.'

Some allusions may have been private jokes shared by the diners, but the only hint of 'ritual eating' lies in PAIN PERDU. If this was 'a society existing entirely for blasphemy' – a verdict few can honestly accept – there was nothing blasphemous in the menus, not a hint of the 'Holy Ghost Pyes' and other diabolical concoctions of the Hell-Fire Club of Wharton's day.

From these diverse and diverting contemporary accounts a clearer picture of the Brotherhood's activities emerges. While not in any way apologizing for their conduct, or seeking to defend their promiscuity in dubious surroundings and circumstances, it seems only fair to point out that there is no evidence of abnormality or even of viciousness by the standards of that age. Emphatically, the 'Monks' were not the depraved perverts conjured up by legend or political prejudice any more than they were 'Black Magicians'.

CHAPTER 5

'PAUL THE AGED'

PAUL WHITEHEAD, who owed his Christian name to the fact that he was born on his saintly namesake's day in 1710, was the son of a Holborn tradesman, Edmund Whitehead.

'No sooner had he learnt to write,' stated his friend and biographer, Captain Thompson, 'than all his letters and requests to his father and family were dressed in Rhime.'

This precocious facility in the use of language was encouraged by his family. They sent their son to be educated under the supervision of a clergyman at Hitchin, where most of his boyhood was spent. His father wanted him to enter commerce and had him apprenticed to a Mercer in the City of London. But commerce and poetry were not a happy combination as far as young Whitehead was concerned. He yearned after freedom from a City desk and thought to achieve it by impetuously bursting into the world of the theatre. Having foolishly backed a bond for £3,000 to a theatrical manager named Fleetwood, he soon discovered the pitfalls of such Thespian adventures. The manager was unable to find the money and Whitehead was committed to the Fleet Prison, which, according to Thompson, 'he bore for years without a sigh'.

Perhaps prison life sharpened his wits, or convinced him that the injustices of this world required a scribe to set them down. At any rate he emerged from prison as a poet with a gift for political satire and a pamphleteer with a genuine talent for stating a case.

He was, as has been said of the Earl of Dorset, 'the best tempered man with the worst tempered Muse'. He attacked all sorts of institutions, first Freemasonry, then the arbitrary actions of the Whig governments. Mrs. Elizabeth Carter, daughter of a Deal clergyman and the most famous blue-stocking of her day, wrote of an encounter with him: 'I must tell you that Mr. Paul Whitehead has been at Deal with a family where I often visit. . . . It was my fate to be once in his company, much against my will, for having naturally as strong an antipathy to wit as some people have to a cat, I at first fairly ran away to avoid it; however, I was dragged in at last . . . to hear part of a satyre ready for the press. Considered as poetry and wit it had some extremely fine strokes, but the vile practice of exalting some characters and abusing others, without any colour of truth or justice, has something so shocking in it that . . . I had much ado . . . to hear it out.'

Like Dashwood, Whitehead was a Tory, but with strong Republican instincts. He had a passion for liberty and what he regarded as the constantly threatened institution of British justice. 'What then,' he stormed, 'is become of the boasted barrier of British Liberty, the *Habeas Corpus Act*? What shall distinguish Britons from those who groan under the most arbitrary governments, if subject to the like oppressions of tyranny?'

Much of this was the bogus rhetoric of a journalistic hack. And, because of this rather than in appreciation of the 'fine strokes' of which Mrs. Carter wrote, he soon won the attention of the Tory Party leaders in Opposition. Quickly he established himself as their paid propagandist, or 'hired hack', as some Whigs preferred to call him. He loved to pull strings behind the scenes, to sit back and plot in some private room in a tavern. Intelligent, witty in a wickedly satirical vein, delighting in perverse paradoxes, he was nevertheless imbued with a very lively independence. One can hardly hurl the epithet 'hired hack' at a man who was a constant attendant at Court and a member of the circle of Frederick, Prince of Wales, when he not only openly declared Republican sentiments, but wrote and published such verses as:

'Well – of all the plagues which make mankind their sport,
Guard me, ye Heav'ns from that worst plague spot – a
  Court.

Midst the mad mansions of Moorfields I'd be
A straw-crown'd monarch in mock majesty,
Rather than Sovereign rule Britannia's fate,
Curs'd with the follies of the farce of State.'

Whitehead's wife, Anna, died when she was quite young and they had no children. One has the impression that he was middle aged before he really settled down to debauchery, though he would only be in his late thirties when the Brotherhood was founded. But it was in his forties and fifties that he started to turn his attention from political satire to light and often rather trite verses which suggest a roué who has suddenly discovered an interest in young girls. It all seems rather ridiculous that a man, when past middle age, should write:

'Ye belles and ye flirts and ye pert little things,
Who trip in this frolicsome round.
Prithee tell me from whence this indecency springs
The sexes at once to confound?'

In this period his verse was full of coy and rather pathetic passion for 'pert little things' whom he was for ever urging to cover up their charms to permit a man's imagination to have full rein. But he linked his love of women with that of the bottle, sonorously proclaiming:

'When Bacchus, jolly God, invites
To revel in his evening rites,
In vain his altars I surround
Though with Burgundian incense crown'd.
No charm has Wine without the Lass,
'Tis Love gives relish to the glass.'

Yet he could also turn his Muse into a cricket-loving bard and go into raptures over a match between Surrey and Kent.

He had a villa on Twickenham Heath, with Bubb Dodington as a neighbour, and it was the latter who introduced him to Dashwood. In many ways he was the antithesis of Francis, but besides belonging to the same party the men found many interests in common and Dashwood proved to be the loyalest friend he ever had. In dedicating his *The Poems and Miscellaneous Compositions of Paul Whitehead* to Dashwood (then Lord le Despencer), Thompson said: 'In you, my Lord, Mr. Whitehead found all that the man of Genius sought, the Friend and Protector. Very few, my Lord, in these days of ignorance and dissipation, are capable of protecting men of genius, or of lamenting their mortal dissolution, like your Lordship.'

When Frederick, Prince of Wales, died suddenly, there was considerable speculation about the efficiency of his medical advisers. It was known that Dr. Thomas Thompson,[1] a friend of Whitehead, had disagreed with the treatment suggested by the Prince's chief doctors. So Whitehead burst into print with:

> 'Though widow'd Julia giggles in her weed,
> Yet who arraigns the Doctor for the deed?
> O'er life and death all absolute his will,
> Right the prescription, whether cure or kill.'

Whitehead was from the first the most enthusiastic supporter of the Brotherhood project. It was he who set about organizing the club and suggesting rules and a code of conduct for members. Where Dashwood talked at random and plucked ideas out of his fertile mind, it was Paul the Aged who moulded them and coaxed the fantasies into some semblance of a constitution. There was about him a bourgeois spirit that was lacking in the other members; he was the middle-class clubman who revelled in pomp and dignity. The more ridiculous of the Brotherhood's solemn ritual can be traced to Whitehead. For a short period in his earlier life he had studied law in the Temple, and he took a lawyer's delight in drawing up a constitution and fashioning it in his own conceits of flowery language.

He has been called the 'Atheist Chaplain' of the Franciscans. In fact, his title was that of High Steward and Treasurer, and in this role he ranked second only to Sir Francis. His misfortunes in youthful financial enterprises,

1. Also Thomson: a memorial to him bore this spelling.

tempered by his sojourn in the Fleet Prison, made him somewhat parsimonious. This trait was revealed in his meticulous treasureship and it was his constant concern that the club should remain solvent. Paul was a forceful treasurer and he personally collected the members' subscriptions. Each member contributed alike, and these subscriptions were intended to pay for both women and wine. But it seems certain that Francis himself generously subsidized the club in more ways than one. Many of the younger members could not have afforded to pay for such luxury as Dashwood and Sandwich desired.[1]

Charles Johnston stated that 'The meetings (of the club) never were protracted beyond a week at a time, nor held oftener than twice a year.' Walpole, on the other hand, suggests the Brothers passed 'two days in every month there'. There may have been some confusion between casual meetings of a few members and the full Chapters of all members, referred to in the wine books. The full Chapters were held not more than twice a year and possibly latterly only once a year. These Chapters were held during the summer, and, judging from the club records, either in June or July.

It is hardly likely that the main meetings of the club were confined to a few weeks each year purely for reasons of economy, as Charles Johnston hinted. Economy of physical strength may have been a more important factor, as two weeks of drinking and wenching must have satiated even these eager sensualists.

Whitehead has been credited with urging Sir Francis to make Medmenham Abbey the headquarters. Apparently he wanted the society to move as far from London as was reasonably possible. And Medmenham was just the type of place to appeal to Francis's peculiar sense of humour; the idea of having a real abbey for the purposes of his burlesque completely captivated him.

About 1160 Hugh de Bolebec II set out on a pilgrimage to the Holy Land and, calling in on the Pope, was advised 'to found an abbey for the remission of his sins'. On his return to England he rebuilt the parish church at Medmen-

1. Churchill and Lloyd were nearly always poverty-stricken.

ham in Buckinghamshire and created an abbey nearby. During the Middle Ages the monks were a riotous and lawless body of men and practised housebreaking in the vicinity with impunity. In 1312 'the Abbot of Medmenham forcibly entered the manor of Dunrugge in Buckinghamshire, felled trees and carried away timber to the value of £100.[1] Doubtless this was born in mind when Henry VIII suppressed the Abbey; at any rate it was dismantled and fell into ruin and the lead was stripped from the roofs and bells and melted down for making guns.

In 1559 James Duffield came to Medmenham and took possession of the Abbey from the Crown. It was later made into a dwelling house without disturbing much of the original fabric, a new E-shaped frontage being added as a compliment to Queen Elizabeth. Eventually Francis Duffield carried out further improvements to the building. A common interest in the fine arts brought together Francis Duffield and Dashwood, who was his neighbour only six miles distant. Before long Duffield was enrolled as a member of the Franciscans and, perhaps before the club was re-established at the Abbey, he invited members to wine and dine there. The prospect must have pleased them; a semi-ruined Cistercian abbey, set mysteriously back from the River Thames amidst 'beautiful hanging woods, meadows and a grove of elms'. Such was Captain Thompson's description of the setting. 'Thither,' wrote Walpole, 'at stated seasons the members adjourned.'

It has been stated that Duffield leased the Abbey to Dashwood personally, after which the former moved to the White House at the top of Ferry Lane. But both the Rev. A. H. Plaisted, an authority on the history of Medmenham, and Walpole claimed it was leased to members of the club, while John Wilkes's version is that 'Sir F—— D——, Sir T—— S——, P—— W—— and other gentlemen to the number of twelve rented the Abbey and often retired there in the summer.' This obviously referred to Dashwood, Sir Thomas Stapleton and Paul Whitehead.

Walpole, after his visit to Medmenham in 1763 described

1. Parish records of Medmenham.

the Abbey as 'built around a small court – the inside of which is covered with ivy, but little or nothing remains that looks conventual. This Abbey is now remarkable by being hired by a set of gentlemen who have erected themselves into a sort of fraternity of Monks. . . . Each has a cell in which indeed there is little more than a bed . . . and into which they may carry women. They have a maid to dress their dinner and clean the house, but no other servants.'

He also referred to the pictures in the 'Common Room of the Abbey', mentioning those of the monarchs of England – 'a piece of paper was pasted over Henry VIII'. This was done, according to some, because that sovereign ordered the dissolution of the monasteries, or, claim others, because he showed scant respect for the lives of his spouses. But what of the paintings of 'Friars and Nuns', which Walpole dismisses cursorily and without explanation? Were these pictures of members and their womenfolk?

One must, however, bear in mind that Walpole visited Medmenham when the Brothers were seriously divided, quarrelling among themselves and near to dissolution. The probable explanation of the lack of servants and the 'very poor accommodation' is that the remaining Franciscans had already disappeared to their new headquarters in the caves at West Wycombe. Certainly other visitors talked of the 'splendour of the Abbey and its sumptuous luxury' as well as creating the impression that there was a whole retinue of servants, and this view is corroborated by the author of *Nocturnal Revels*.

Presumably Walpole had been well acquainted with the rumours about the Brotherhood, and went down to Medmenham to snoop. Perhaps the Brothers expected him and therefore removed all traces of luxury and opulence to the caves, so that what Walpole tells us is a second-hand version. For a writer usually so prolific and fond of detail his account of Medmenham is brief and unsatisfactory. Nor does it quite come up to Walpole's usual style; some of the phrases are full of ill-chosen words and one gets the impression that the whole description is merely a few rough notes hurriedly linked together. It is just possible, however, that Walpole himself may have fallen into temptation at Medmenham, if not to the extent of being made a member (which is highly unlikely) at least to have joined in the revels. He was an assiduous letter writer and many of his visits to country houses were retailed in vividly descriptive prose in his personal correspondence. But the account from which I have quoted was never mentioned in any of Walpole's correspondence and was only published years afterwards.[1]

But one must admit that Walpole's statements are mostly confirmed by other sources. He tells us that the Brothers had pegs in the Abbey Common Room on which to hang their habits. Over each peg was inscribed the Christian name and place of abode of each 'Monk'. That the Brothers wore monkish habits, as some have suggested, is not borne out by Walpole. 'The habit is more like a waterman's than a monk's,' he commented, 'and consists of white hat, white jacket, white trousers. The Prior, (this would be Dashwood) has a red hat like a Cardinal's and a red bonnet turned up with coney skin.'

Yet the Rev. A. H. Plaisted mentions that 'the badge of the Order' was a costume of crimson and blue with a silver badge, and that the words 'Love and Friendship' were inscribed 'on the mitre and on the gown'. This badge is similarly described by Wilkes, but he calls it a brooch and rather suggests that it was worn only by the 'Ladies, who were dressed up as nuns and allowed to wear masks'.

Like all the early Cistercian churches the Abbey was towerless. The initial cost of adapting it to a club headquarters was borne by Dashwood. His zest for showmanship caused him to exchange the plain windows for stained glass and to build the pseudo-ruins of a tower on to the south-east corner of the building. The original Abbey had neither statuary nor pictures, its only ornamentation being an image of the Virgin seated on a throne and holding the infant Jesus in her arms. This Dashwood removed, placing it in a niche in the tower. This act may be significant not of Dashwood's contempt for religion, but of his concern to dissociate pagan practices from religious statues. There was

1. *Journals of Visits to Country Seats* (Walpole).

no attempt to use the statue for any blasphemous rites or to desecrate it in any way. It was placed in the unused tower in an orthodox and reverent manner.

Dashwood brought Nicholas Revett over to Medmenham to help plan the alterations to the Abbey. Everything was carried out in great secrecy, including the adaptation of the Common Room and fitting out of the cells. Workmen were hired from London, and, so as to avoid any gossip locally, taken back there each night.

Years before, when Dashwood had travelled in France, he had delighted to read the stories of Rabelais, especially those of Pantagruel and Gargantua. Remembering this, he borrowed from Rabelais the motto over the Abbey of Thélème and had it painted over the eastern porch of the house:

'FAY CE QUE VOUDRAS' (Do as you please)

But he did more than just borrow the motto of the imaginary abbey on the banks of the Loire; he drew freely from Rabelais's own code for Thélème. Gargantua's religious order was to be 'contrary to all others', and the Franciscans were certainly founded on the same principle. So identical in many ways were the two codes of conduct – that of Medmenham and that of Thélème – that here is ample proof that the source of Dashwood's inspiration was essentially in Rabelais and not in Rosicrucianism or black magic. Reference to *The Works of Rabelais*, Book I, Chapters LI to LVII shows more clearly than anything else that the stories of black magic and satanism are very wide of the mark.

Gargantua laid down that the Abbey of Thélème should have neither clock nor dial and that 'all hours should be disposed of . . . for the greatest loss of time that I know is, to count the hours'. Rabelais made great play with the word *horae* and so did the Franciscans. John Hall Stevenson spoke of the latter's punning on *horae* – pronouncing it as in Latin, but spelling it with a 'w' in front of the 'h'. So the brothers banished *horae* as a phrase suggesting time, but gave the word its legendary meaning of three female figures. Captain Thompson expressed this in his *Temple of Venus*:

> 'The winds took pity on the little whore,
> And kindly puff'd her to the Cyprian shore;
> The circling HORAE saw the floating car
> And kindly sav'd her, for the God of War.
> Eunomia, Dica and Irene fair[1]
> Made the sweet baby their peculiar care:
> Taught her the deepest mysteries of love,
> Then bore the Beauty to the powers above.'

Gargantua again ordained that 'into this religious order should be admitted no women that were not fair, well featured, and of a sweet disposition; nor men that were not comely, personable and well-conditioned'. And instead of the three vows of chastity, poverty and obedience for the nuns, '... in this convent they might be honourably married, rich and live at liberty'. Undoubtedly Thélème was the model for Medmenham.

The sentiments of Rabelais were those of Dashwood:

> 'Here enter not, religious boobies, sots,
> Impostors, sniveling hypocrites, bigots;
> Dark-brain distorted owls, worse than the Huns
> Or Ostrogots; fore-runners of baboons:
> Curs'd snakes, dissembling varlets, seeming sancts,
> Slipshod caffards, beggars pretending wants;
> Fomentors of divisions and debates,
> Elsewhere, not here, make sale of your deceits.
> Your filthy trumperies,
> Stuff'd with pernicious lies.
>   (Not worth a bubble)
> Would only trouble
> Our earthly Paradise.'

In the Abbey grounds were introduced many Rabelaisian touches. A small temple dedicated to Cloacina[2] bore the inscription: 'The chapel of ease was founded in the year

1. The names of the *Horae*.
2. Goddess of the Sewers.

1760', while above the entrance were carved the words: 'ABQUE PAUPERIBUS PRODEST, LOCUPLETIBUS ABQUE; ABQUE NEGLECTUM PUERIS SENIBUS NOCEBIT' (Alike it benefits the poor, alike the rich; Alike, when slighted, it will harm youths and old men).

While the club had many members, only about a dozen attended regularly at the Chapters and these constituted an 'Inner Circle', or Superior Order. Walpole said that 'there are two Orders of Friars, a Superior, comprising the Apostles, and an Inferior, including visitors and those not yet elected to the inner councils of the Order'. There were twelve Apostles in the Superior Order, with Francis at their head as Prior of the Abbey, but there is no foundation for the assertion of Johnston that they ridiculed the Christian Apostles and assumed their names. W. Bolton in an article in the *Ex-Libris Journal* of April 1901 said that 'a Saint Andrew, Saint Denys, Saint David and Saint George were among them'. No authority for this statement is provided. The titles the Brothers used were usually their own Christian names with their place of residence or birth added on to it. By mere coincidence the names of many of them . . . Francis, Thomas, John and Paul . . . were the same as those of either Apostles or Saints.

The club records imply that the twelve Apostles elected an 'Abbot' each year, but Wilkes said that the role of 'Abbot of the Day was taken in rotation, the appointed one ordering the feasts and programme for the day. He also has first choice of the women.' Possibly, if the Chapters lasted about a fortnight, this is to some extent correct, as such procedure would give each Apostle and the Prior a chance of dictating the proceedings. 'Do as you please' perhaps proved an impracticable motto for these pleasure-seekers and so an 'Abbot of the Day' was appointed to prevent any anarchical tendencies.

There were great differences in age of the various members, and possibly the precedence which seniority gave the elder Apostles created a sense of frustration and jealousy among the younger 'Inferior' members. Churchill in particular was angered by Whitehead's seniority and they appear to have clashed violently on the choice of women. In verse Churchill constantly lampooned Whitehead. 'From the writings of Churchill,' wrote Captain Thompson, 'one would conclude that he had a very particular enmity to Paul Whitehead, but to do him justice he had enmity to no man; very few breasts have breathed more philanthropy, charity and honour.'

Once one starts to delve into the secret rites of the Brotherhood, it is like getting lost in a maze. Contemporary figures have obscured the truth in a welter of imagination. 'No servants were permitted in the chapel of the monastery,' says Charles Johnston, 'as the very decorations of it would have betrayed their secrets. . . . Figures on the ceiling representing actions and attitudes horrible to imagine. . . . The diffidence and conscious guilt made them (*the Brothers*) even distrust each other till bound to secrecy by oaths and imprecations.'

John Wilkes added to this picture by saying: 'No profane eye has dared to penetrate into the English Eleusinian Mysteries of the Chapter Room, where the monks assembled on solemn occasions . . . secret rites performed and libations to the *Bona Dea*. . . . At the end of the passage over the door was AUDE HOSPES CONTEMNERE OPES.' He, too, spoke of the ceiling 'glittering with unspeakable frescoes'.

Churchill has been mentioned as Johnston's chief source of information about Medmenham when he wrote *Chrysal*. It is generally believed that his references to 'my Master' in *Chrysal* are intended for Churchill. But he described 'my Master' as being elected to the 'inner circle' and, although the Rev. A. H. Plaisted included Wilkes, Churchill and Lloyd as members of the Superior Order, it is doubtful whether any of them were and almost certain that Churchill and Lloyd were not. Johnston's patron was Lord Mount Edgecumbe,[1] a naval officer working under Sandwich at the Admiralty, and he may have obtained third-hand information from this source. Sandwich was one of the Apostles. This should be considered in assessing the following account by Johnston of an initiation ceremony:

1. Dashwood and Mount Edgecumbe corresponded.

'My master, then clad in a milk-white robe and finest linen that flowed loosely round him, repaired at the tolling of the bell to the chapel, knocking thrice upon the door. It was opened to him and the sound of soft and solemn music was heard. On his entrance he made a most profound obeisance and advanced slowly towards a table that stood against the wall at the upper end of the chapel.

'As soon as he came to the rails, by which it was surrounded, he fell upon his knees, and making a profession of his principles nearly in the words, but with the most gross perversion of the sense of the Articles of Faith of the religion established in the country, demanded admission within the rails.'

Johnston then told how the 'twelfth place' at the rails was vacant; there were, he said, 'two competitors for admission' and, after a prayer delivered in mimic solemnity, 'my master was elected'.

After the election ceremony there was 'a banquet in the chapel, both Superiors and Inferiors vying with each other in loose songs and dissertations of lewdness'. If, as Wilkes, Walpole and others have said, none but a Superior could enter the chapel, this is an inaccurate picture. Equally distorted are the lurid accounts of black magic and satanism conjured up by other writers. Wraxhall was one of the worst offenders in exaggerating the excesses of the Brotherhood. He spoke of 'black baptisms, the sprinkling of salt and sulphur' and the satanic paraphernalia of 'inverted crucifixes, black tapers, and blood-red triangular wafers'. No authority on black magic has yet been able to establish any positive evidence that satanism was practised in the club, nor demonstrated that any occult symbols were used. The possession by Sir Francis of books on the black arts, his passion for Rosicrucian lamps are no proof at all. Practitioners of the black arts invariably make extensive use of signs and symbols in any building or place where they operate, but, though both the gardens of the Abbey and those of West Wycombe House, were liberally strewn with temples to mythological goddesses and gods, nowhere was there any vestige of occult symbolism either at Medmenham or in the caves. Nor is there any confirmation of the ridiculous story that the Brothers drank wine out of human skulls.

Whitehead had a remarkable talent for upsetting people, though he and Dashwood seem to have got on together admirably. He could never resist tilting at the Court, which he despised, and as a result of his satire *Manners*, in which he criticized the servility of courts in general, he was arrested, tried for libel and once again imprisoned. In the club he was disliked by some of the members because of his exploitation of the privileges of seniority. Robert Lloyd, friend and ally of Churchill, dubbed him as 'learned in lechery, a sedulous and patient seducer and a veritable troubadour of blasphemy'. He was usually the author of the Brotherhood's obscene hymns. Plaintively he would intone to the assembled Brothers:

'Why on me then, alone, should your vengeance thus fall?
Why not Thomas, or Francis as well as Saint Paul?
On Aylesbury John why your anger not place,
Who all must allow is so brim-full of grace?

But Francis would never hear a word against Paul, and, after he was created Baron le Despencer in 1763, he rewarded Whitehead with a pension of £800 a year and provided him with a home in West Wycombe House. There, while the new baron went abroad in his handsome coach bearing the motto *Pro Magna Charta*, Whitehead lived in scholarly seclusion, still undoubtedly an active member of the club, but, as both men grew older, tending to spend his nights quietly by the fireside, reading to his patron. Benjamin Franklin wrote of Whitehead 'rising early to collect the London papers', which he read diligently from page to page, marking certain paragraphs which later he would relate to Franklin and his host.

On 30 December, 1774, Whitehead passed away after a long and often painful illness. His biographer, Thompson, as well as Langley, testified that he burnt a large quantity of his papers before he died. Thus some of the most valuable data on the Brotherhood was destroyed, and by this act, far from silencing rumour and malicious reports, he fanned the flames which fed them.

It is not easy to assess this strange character, nor to separate his virtues and vices. Here was a lecher who nevertheless 'behaved kindly to his idiot wife'; a supporter of Frederick, Prince of Wales, yet a violent Republican prepared to risk jail for expressing such sentiments; a composer of profane hymns and obscene verses, yet a rather naïve sentimentalist in other moods; a cynical, disillusioned roué, yet one who could either perpetrate a grim jest or display pathetic loyalty to an old friend when he composed his will:

'I give to the Right Honourable Francis, Baron le Despencer, my heart aforesaid, together with £50 to be laid out in the purchase of a marble urn in which I desire it may be deposited and placed, if his Lordship pleases, in some corner of his mausoleum as a memorial of its owner's warm attachment to the noble founder.'

Francis fulfilled the request, though whether the pomp and pageantry he summoned up for the funeral was a genuine tribute to his old friend, or another of his practical jokes is open to questions. The heart was duly put in an urn with the inscriptions:

PAUL WHITEHEAD, ESQ.,
of Twickenham.

Obiit Dec. 30, 1774.

Unhallowed hands this urn forebear,
No gems nor orient spoil
Lie here conceal'd – but what's more rare,
A HEART, that knew no guile.

A company of the Bucks Militia was paraded for the ceremony of depositing the poet's heart in the mausoleum. According to contemporary accounts the militiamen, bearing the heart in its yellow urn, marched round the grounds of West Wycombe House, up the hill to the Church of St.

Lawrence and then 'three times round the mausoleum' before the urn was deposited in its niche. There was a band of flutes, fifes and drums and a choir in attendance and the oratorio of *Goliah* was played in the church to mark the occasion.

But the villagers were shocked at such ostentation and lost no time in retailing to visitors the story of Whitehead's 'evil influence' over their Squire and telling them that if only they could see the heart 'it would appear as black in death as it had been in life'. For years afterwards people from far and wide climbed the hill to the mausoleum to view the heart, which was taken from its urn and shown to them. By 1839 it must have been a repulsive, shrivelled-up and withered object – 'about the size of a walnut'[1] was one description. But this did not deter some ghoulish curio hunter from removing the object from the urn and walking away with it sometime during that year.

And that was the last that was heard of the heart of Paul Whitehead, though his memory is still preserved in a bust in the pillared hall at West Wycombe House.

1. *Gentleman's Magazine.*

CHAPTER 6

THE MONKS OF MEDMENHAM

IT is impossible to trace all the members of the Order of 'Saint' Francis. Probably at the most there were no more than fifty, at the least about thirty-five.

Even the identity of all the Twelve Apostles is a matter of conjecture. Allowing for the fact that Dashwood was not counted in the twelve, one can say with certainty that they included Paul Whitehead, George Bubb Dodington, Sir Thomas Stapleton, John Montagu, fourth Earl of Sandwich, Thomas Potter, Francis Duffield, Sir William Stanhope, Sir John Dashwood-King, Mr. Clarke of Henley and Robert Vansittart. But who were the other two? Possibly Joseph Borgnis, who seems to have had something to do with the resuscitation of the club after it moved to Medmenham, and Dr. Benjamin Bates.

The most significant feature of the membership was not that all of them were rakes – indeed, several were not – but that each man had some claim to distinction in his own right, quite apart from birth. None was a nonentity, not even the podgy, futile figure of Dodington. In politics, in art, in literature, in scholastic attainments the club had representatives; few other societies of the day could boast of so many learned and intelligent members. And doubtless there was keen competition to join; perhaps some of those who tried and failed were among the bitterest and most vituperative critics of the Order.

Whitehead, Dodington, Sir Thomas Stapleton and Sir William Stanhope were the most senior members. Of these, Dodington was the least likeable. He was well over sixty when he became a member and the sight of this obese, waddling, puffy-faced peer chasing the wenches in the gardens of Medmenham was the subject of much malicious fun for such political opponents as Wilkes and Churchill.

George Bubb Dodington had been born plain George Bubb and, snob that he was, had added on the name of Dodington, a slightly superior relative by birth.

'Bubb is his name and bubbies doth he chase,
This swollen bullfrog with lascivious face.'

This was the sharp-tongued Churchill speaking. He regarded Dodington as the most contemptible place-hunter in England, a man who performed so many political acrobatics that no one could ever be sure on whose side he stood. Yet Dodington was not without a pawky humour, possessed of the saving grace of being able to laugh at himself and never appearing to mind being made a butt. Frederick, Prince of Wales, borrowed money from him and then laughed at him for being an old fool, boxing his ears and rolling him downstairs, while the Queen openly sniggered when he burst the seams of his trousers as he bowed before her.

All his political life and even after he was made Lord Melcombe he acted as go-between for favour-hunters and ambitious men jockeying for office. Yet he, like Whitehead, was proof of the extraordinary loyalty which Dashwood could command from his closest friends. When he died he left £500 to 'Lord le Despencer . . . for building an arch temple column or additional room' to house his ashes. It was typical of the man's perpetual love of pomp and his fussy self-importance. He died in July 1762 before the political dissensions which rent the club into warring factions. Lord le Despencer honoured his wish. Choosing a site on the crest of West Wycombe Hill beside the Church of St. Lawrence, he built a mausoleum consisting of a hexagonal wall without a roof, 150 yards in circumference, with twelve Tuscan columns. The knapped flint walls, the iron grilles in the arches round which the ivy has wound its way, the gaps in the wall housing birds' nests, the long grass and wild strawberries give to the mausoleum today that appearance of melancholy and decay in which the pre-romantics of the eighteenth century delighted. And on the wall Dodington's name was carved and his effigy set in one of the niches.

Of a totally different character was John Montagu, Earl of Sandwich, the friend of Dashwood's youth and fellow member of the Divan Club. 'The most vicious of the Monks of Medmenham, as lecherous as a goat' is one description of him. Horace Walpole drily observed that 'Sandwich can never get rid of the smell of brimstone'. His mother was said to have dreamed shortly before his birth that she would bear a beast whose foreparts were those of a monkey, the hindparts those of a goat.

It is true that he was ugly, but rather in the style of a capering satyr. However, unprepossessing he might appear to men, for women he had an irresistible fascination. For the Sandwich legend he had only himself to blame; more than any other of the Brothers he was a rake in the Roaring Boy tradition, a tempestuous, rampaging roisterer in the Restoration mould. He would have fitted admirably into the age of Rochester. His sexual progress ranged from the stews of Drury Lane to the boudoirs of the most beautiful and illustrious women of the realm. He flitted from one amorous interlude to another, organizing Cyprian parties at Mrs. Hayes's bagnio, winning the favour of Fanny Murray, the most fabulous courtesan of her day, and finally losing his favourite mistress, Martha Ray, when she was shot outside Covent Garden by a love-crazed clergyman.

For a short period after his marriage it seemed as though even this arch-rake had reformed. For two years he was not to be seen around the taverns he had always haunted and there were no more boudoir adventures. Then, after the birth of her first child, Lady Sandwich's health broke down and her mind became unhinged. Her husband reverted to his natural role.

In his pursuit of Venus he fought a score of duels, terrorizing his rivals to such an extent that one of them, Lord Mountford, begged to be allowed to hide beneath the petticoats of Kitty Fisher, Sandwich's mistress, when news was brought of the unexpected arrival of the turbulent earl at her apartments.

In 1760 Sandwich met the great love of his life, Martha Ray, a girl in her teens who worked in a shop in St. John

Lane. He seduced her, had her educated as a singer – he had a passion for music – and settled her at Hinchingbrooke, where she bore him nine children. Nineteen years later Hackman, a renegade clergyman who had nurtured a hopeless love for the charming singer, shot her and paid the penalty at the scaffold. Sandwich was overwhelmed: 'I could have borne anything but this,' he moaned.

Yet, despite his ceaseless quest for pleasure, his wenching and drinking, Sandwich devoted himself to public work with surprising ardour. A hard taskmaster not only to others but to himself as well, he brought to the office of First Lord of the Admiralty a restless drive combined with a courageous ruthlessness. One of the most hated men in the country, he never allowed this reputation to worry him; his serene arrogance protected him from the sneers and barbs of politicians. At the Admiralty he worked long hours, not even leaving his desk to dine out. Instead he sent messengers to bring him a slice of meat which he ate between two chunks of bread, thus giving his own name to the sandwich. Probably posperity owes him more for this than the fact that a group of Pacific islands was also named after him.

Like Dashwood, he had a contempt for superstition and a vehement dislike of Popery. He was said to hold burlesque services in a village church, preaching blasphemous sermons to a congregation of cats, and keeping a baboon for a 'chaplain'. Once when he produced the baboon and called for it to 'say grace', a clergyman guest drily remonstrated: 'My Lord, I was intending to offer grace myself, but I had no idea you had a near relative for a chaplain.'

But these are legends and, though often quoted against Sandwich, may be as wildly exaggerated as those surrounding Medmenham. If one is to discuss Sandwich's lesser recreations, it may be more charitable to mention that he was also an accomplished player on the kettle-drums and a competent cricketer, frequently caricatured flourishing a bat. In short, he was one of the least likeable, but at the same time one of the most spectacular members of the Brotherhood.

The Duffield family, most of whom lived around Medmenham, provided at least two and probably three of the Brothers. Francis Duffield, who died in 1728, had four sons, Edmund, Francis, James and John. Of these Francis and James were almost certainly members. The former, an army officer and accomplished painter, leased the Abbey to the Franciscans and continued to visit it afterwards. He was 'a bold, gallant gentleman and of a temperament which promises a long life', according to a handwritten comment on a manuscript taken from behind some wainscoting in a room at Medmenham Abbey. This MS., dated 1748, contains some interesting pen pictures of the Duffields.

The prophecy of a long life for Francis was not fulfilled. He died at the age of thirty-nine in 1758, according to Medmenham Parish records, though another source gives the date as 1755 and his age then as twenty-six.

The manuscript found at Medmenham has this to say about James Duffield: 'James is an idle, drunken fellow, has run thro' almost all his fortune and, tho' a brilliant wit and excellent scholar, spends his time among a set of scoundrels in an alehouse.' This was probably the Dog and Badger public house nearby.

Edmund is described as 'a man of exceeding weak constitution'. He took holy orders and had the living of Medmenham presented to him by his brother, Francis. Thomas Langley, quoting from the parish records, lists him as Vicar of Medmenham until 11 April, 1749, when he was 'drowned at Newlock' in the Thames. It has been suggested that he was overcome with remorse after joining the Franciscans and that he deliberately took his life, but of this there is no clear proof.

One of the earliest members was Thomas Potter, Paymaster-General and son of an Archbishop of Canterbury. Having inherited £100,000 from his father, he proceeded to spend it on orgy upon orgy so that it was written of him:

'He drank with drunkards, liv'd with sinners.
Herded with infidels for dinners.'

For a short period Potter was secretary to the Prince of Wales, and he also held office as Vice-Treasurer for Ireland.

In the House of Commons he made effortlessly scintillating speeches with a nonchalant cynicism. Outside it he devoted himself wholeheartedly to the pursuit of debauchery. It followed not unnaturally that he was one of the most fervent of the Brotherhood and, with Whitehead, provided the words for most of Dashwood's 'psalms', none of which are fit for publication. Enemies of Potter said he was 'the chief priest of necromancy in Dashwood's Temple', but it was something half way between necromancy and necrophilia which Potter practised. He was neither as foolish as to dabble in black magic, nor as perverse as to conceive a passion for corpses in the manner of Baudelaire. But he had that morbid fascination for the trappings of death which from the earliest times has been a will-o'-the-wisp for debauchers. Mostly this was indulged to the extent of mingling with the mobs who went to see executions, but he was sufficiently a patron of the macabre to prefer his debauchery in surroundings that suggested a tomb. It may well have been Potter who pointed the way to the caves at West Wycombe as the ideal, the ultimate, the perfect headquarters for the Franciscans. But, as he died at the age of forty in 1759, it is by no means certain that he lived to see this realized.

Potter also shared the dislike felt by the younger members of the society for Bubb Dodington (Lord Melcombe Regis). He wrote:

> 'Titles with me are vain, and nothing worth.
> I reverence virtue, but laugh at birth.
> To think a Melcombe worth my last regards
> Is treason to the majesty of bards.'

It was Potter who introduced that political *enfant terrible*, John Wilkes, to the Brotherhood. But it was only shortly before Potter's death that Wilkes actually became one of the Brothers. Potter had long been his evil genius, and, though not influencing him politically, actively encouraged him in the pursuit of lechery, urging him that 'if you prefer young women and whores to old women and wives, come to Bath, and indulge the heavenly inspired passion of Lust'.

Wilkes, next to Dashwood and Whitehead, was perhaps the most significant of the 'Monks' and for this reason merits a whole chapter to himself.

Of the other senior members Sir William Stanhope was son of the Earl of Chesterfield and Robert Vansittart (possibly a member of the 'Inner Circle') was a Regius Professor at Oxford University. The Vansittart family of Shottesbrooke provided three 'Monks'. Besides Robert there were Arthur, a Berkshire M.P., and Henry, who was Governor of Bengal. It has been argued that Henry could not have been a member as he was in India from 1755–63, when the society was operating most actively. Nevertheless Henry was almost certainly one of the earliest members. Proof of this lies in the fact that his portrait as a 'Monk of Medmenham' was painted by William Hogarth in 1753. Whether he rejoined the society on his return from India is uncertain, but this friend of Clive and vigorous administrator has left many legends of his activities at Medmenham. It is said that he presented a baboon to the club, which he shipped over from India, and requested that it be dressed up as a chaplain. There is confirmation from various sources that he presented the baboon to the Brotherhood, but the story that it was dressed up as a chaplain (as will be explained later) is either a figment of the imagination of Charles Johnston, or else a confused version of the story about Lord Sandwich's baboon.

Sir Richard Burton suggested rather obscurely that Henry Vansittart introduced the teachings of *Kama Sutra* to Medmenham, and, if this is so, it would explain at least some of the strange rites of the society. The *Kama Sutra* of Vatsayana is one of the most remarkable of all Sanskrit works and may well be one of the eldest and, despite its Ovidian amorality, one of the sanest text-books on sex ever compiled. It is not a pornographic work as some modern writers claim; it would be truer to say that it was originally written in a dialect that ceased to be spoken centuries ago, and it is in the adaptation of the work that translators have shown an Anglo-Saxon crudeness and lack of perception in their choice of words. Sir Richard Burton said of it: 'The

Kama Sutra has stood the test of centuries and has placed Vatsayana among the immortals.'

Hogarth was another member, and doubtless the creator of *The Rake's Progress* found in the Monks of Medmenham not only the gay, fantastic round and Bacchanalian dance, but a medium for sly satires on:

> 'There was old Proteus coming from the sea,
> And wreathed Triton blew his winding horn.'

For Hogarth certainly decked up the wayward monks in mock-classical solemnity, exploiting subtly their foibles and weaknesses.

Not all the members were such incorrigible lechers as Sandwich and Potter. Some, like Clarke of Henley, Richard Hopkins, a wealthy landowner, and Sir John D'Aubrey[1] were upright men both in their public and private life. None of these, except perhaps Clarke, did much more than use the club for a convivial evening's wining and dining. Sir John D'Aubrey was a magistrate – 'one of the best and most incorruptible of his age'.

The Earl of Bute was the sole Prime Minister to have belonged to this fraternity, though it is doubtful whether he visited the Abbey often. The most unpopular minister who ever held office, he was disliked by most of the Brothers, not merely by the Whigs, but by some Tories as well. 'This damned Scotsman,' as Churchill called him, was always suspected of being a Jacobite in disguise, and his presence at Medmenham caused much dissension.

More regular attenders were Dr. Benjamin Bates, Dashwood's doctor, Henry Lovibond Collins, a poet who was sometimes referred to as 'Mr. Lovibond', and George Selwyn, the wit who was rusticated at Oxford for alleged blasphemy.

George Augustus Selwyn has been described by Walter Jerrold as 'the first recognized society wit'. Dr. Warner, his biographer, said of him:

1. Lipscombe, in his *History of Buckinghamshire*, claimed that D'Aubrey had admitted to being a member, but that he was 'too young' to join the 'Inner Circle.'

> 'Social wit which, never kindling strife,
> Blazed in the small, sweet courtesies of life.'

He possessed in a high degree that common characteristic of the Brotherhood – a dislike of Popery. He always claimed that the act for which he was rusticated at Oxford was not blasphemy, but 'an astringent satire on Rome' – his use of a communion chalice at a wine party.

Selwyn entered Parliament in 1747 at the age of twenty-eight, and remained a member for more than thirty years. But his wit was reserved for social life and not the House of Commons, where his attendances in the lobbies were not as numerous as his appearances at public executions, for which, like Potter, he had a passion. He was also famed for his punmanship and ready retorts, but the latter lose much of their savour when detached from the context of the eighteenth century. When Lord North was married in the summer of 1751 somebody said that it was very hot weather in which to marry so fat a bride. 'Oh,' replied Selwyn, 'she was kept in ice for three days before.' And when a fellow member met Selwyn as he was leaving the House of Commons one day, he inquired: 'What, is the House up?' 'No,' replied Selwyn, 'but Burke is.'

Of the lesser-known members Giuseppe Borgnis was by far the closest to Dashwood and a study of his paintings reveals how minutely and faithfully he reproduced the ideas, the satires and the fantasies of his patron. Borgnis had been painting for many years in the area around his native valley near Milan, both on the Italian and Swiss sides of the border, until Dashwood discovered him. He did an enormous amount of work in Craveggia, where it is still much admired, but his life in England from 1751 to 1761 is to a large extent wrapped in mystery. His paintings at West Wycombe House show the influence of the Cinquecento and Seicento, chiefly Raphael, Caracci and Guido Reni; they are masterpieces in the sheer poetry of colour. Though it is certain that he started the chancel painting of the Last Supper at the Church of St. Lawrence and that the design for this was entirely his, the painting must have been finished by his son, Giovanni, who continued to work at West Wycombe and was actually paid £100 for this task. For in 1761 Giuseppe Borgnis had a fatal fall from his scaffold, whether by accident or the design of jealous rivals is unknown. An interesting point is that just by Borgnis's house in Marlow there is a curious cave, much smaller than that at West Wycombe, but suggesting that at some time or other it was used as a meeting place. It might well be that Borgnis had something to do with the work under the hill at West Wycombe, possibly some of the carvings or original interior decoration there were his work. It was just about the time that he arrived in England – 1751 – that work on the caves was begun.

George, third Earl of Oxford, a relative of Horace Walpole, Henry Fox (Lord Holland), Sir Francis Delaval, Simon Luttrell and John Fane, Earl of Westmorland, are all reputed to have been members. Walpole claimed that Evelyn Pierrepont, Duke of Kingston, and John Manners, Marquis of Granby, were elected to the society, probably in the early 'sixties.

Some of the so-called poets who were members were little more than competent imitators of Dryden, confining their choice of subjects to smut. But one who was capable of rising to the greatest heights in verse composition and who deserves to be better known today was Charles Churchill, the gangling, awkward rake and rebel, a dissolute, renegade clergyman who nevertheless had in his make-up a spark of warm-hearted idealism unique among his contemporaries. Had Churchill entered politics early in life, he might well have achieved as great a success as Wilkes, his friend, for throughout his brief life he took politics seriously.

Churchill was forced into the Church by his father. In the latter's curacy at Rainham he 'pray'd and starved on £40 a year'. Struggling to provide a mere existence for a wife and two children, he brewed cider and carried on an illicit trade with the villagers. These early years broke Churchill's heart, though not his spirit. When his father died, he severed all links with the Church and began in earnest his Rake's Progress.

But he was a rebel even in his debauchery. He scorned women of quality and preferred to rampage in lowlier company with Wilkes than to conquer society. He even preferred beer to wine, which may have been one reason for his never settling down happily in the company of the Brothers. In politics he allied himself with Wilkes in his fight against George III's personal rule. Despite his dissipations, he was one of the kindest-hearted of men, a loyal friend and a courageous fighter for the things in which he passionately believed. He foresaw the need for a more sympathetic approach to the people of the North American colonies and urged that they should be given more freedom; in many respects he was well in advance of his age in political thought. Today his works are better appreciated in the U.S.A. than in Britain. He is, perhaps, the most underrated poet of his century.

Just as Thomas Potter was Wilkes's evil genius, so Wilkes was Churchill's. He delighted in encouraging his friend to explore the not-always-primrose path to revelry: 'If you will wait, you shall kiss the lips – if you will dine, you shall suck the sweetest bubbies of this hemisphere' is a typical example of some of Wilkes's letters to Churchill.

In November 1764 Churchill arrived in Boulogne on his way to visit Wilkes in Paris. There was a prolonged drinking session in an *auberge* and on the fourth of the month, worn out by excesses, Churchill died. He was only thirty-two. Yet, even in this short life the poet had established a reputation for himself. A contemporary report of his death mentioned that 'all the English ships in Boulogne harbour struck their colours in honour of the greatest satirist of the day'.

Churchill's death came as a mortal blow to his other great friend, Robert Lloyd, also a member of the Medmenhamites. Broken-hearted, Lloyd declared: 'From now on I have nothing to live for. I shall follow poor Charles.' He took to his bed and within a few months was dead. Such was the devotion which Charles Churchill inspired among his friends, and, as Captain Thompson freely and generously admitted, even his enemies saw his good points.

Lloyd was the son of a Welshman, a master at Westminster School, where he was educated along with Churchill, Cowper and Warren Hastings. He was captain of the school, had a brilliant career at Cambridge and returned to Westminster as bursar. Never particularly happy in this post, he eventually gave it up to seek a living as a writer. But, though for a time he edited the *St. James's Magazine*, he never made a financial success of his new profession, and his debaucheries with Churchill did not help matters. He had undoubted talent, but lacked originality. Wilkes said of him: 'His peculiar excellence was the dressing up of an old thought in a new manner. He was content to scamper round the foot of Parnassus on his Welsh pony.'

After a prolonged fight against poverty Lloyd was arrested for debt and sent to the Fleet Prison. Churchill rallied round him nobly, dispatching some money and food to his friend, but his attempt to raise enough funds to buy Lloyd out of jail failed. None of the other Medmenhamites seems to have come to Lloyd's rescue. In his last months he was nursed by Churchill's sister, Patty, to whom he was supposed to have been betrothed. Ironically, success came to him on his deathbed: his comic opera, *The Capricious Lovers*, was then performed at Drury Lane.

Other members are more shadowy when it comes to identifying them. Who, for example, was 'Brother John of York'? It may well have been John Hall Stevenson, as from his known association with Dashwood and various sly disclosures in his works, it would seem that he must have joined the Franciscans at some period or other. Of more interest, however, is the riddle of whether he joined this society simply to spy on the members and to obtain evidence against Dashwood, for of all the barbs against the Brotherhood those of Hall Stevenson are the most scurrilous.

Stevenson was a bigoted Whig, a fanatical opponent of Lord Bute and had a witch-hunting obsession against Jacobites and Roman Catholics. He was for ever imagining there was a Jacobite or a Jesuit underneath every Tory's bed. In 1745 he was so convinced that Prince Charles Edward's invasion of England threatened 'Popish dominion over all Britain' that he formed a 'flying squadron' of horsemen to check the invader. This is a fair measure of his fanaticism when one considers the indifference with which most Britons greeted the southward march of the Prince and his Highland legions. Again, when Lord Bute paid a visit to Rome, Stevenson believed that there was a secret plot to restore Popery to England, and, like the majority of the Brothers, he ranted against what he called 'the Pagan Church of Rome'.

This friend of Lawrence Sterne and author of *Crazy Tales*, however, was so narrow in his outlook that he feared even a burlesque of Catholicism might result in its participants acquiring a liking for 'pernicious ritual'. After a visit to Medmenham in June 1762 he wrote to Paul Whitehead (and in similar vein to Wilkes), saying: 'I do not believe there is anything miraculous in the Shrine of Saint Francis . . . but say a Mass for me!' It was a sneering jest. But, though dreading 'pernicious ritual', it was sheer hypocrisy for Stevenson to pretend that the society's activities had 'no interest for me'.[1] His own Demoniacs' Club was a feeble imitation of the Franciscans.

Later, he sought to denigrate Dashwood and the Franciscans in various obnoxious verses, but here again the motive seems to have been mainly political spite. No one has attempted to ascertain the identity of the anonymous author of *Nocturnal Revels*, who described himself on the fly-leaf of this book as 'a Monk of the Order of St. Francis'. The book was published in 1779, which rules out most of the older members of the Brotherhood, who were dead by then. It is certain it wasn't Dashwood, who died only two years later. It could have been Stevenson, who not only used pseudonyms for his work, but had the same habit as the Nocturnal Reveller of dedicating his books to himself. Yet the style of writing is too straightforward for this imitator of Rabelais, and it is all in prose, whereas Stevenson could not resist breaking into verse and quoting passage after passage from the classics. And again, the narrative is almost too favourable to the society to have emanated from Stevenson's pen. There are some grounds for believing that it may have been

1. Correspondence with Wilkes.

the work of John Wilkes, or at least a Wilkesian-inspired work produced by one of his cronies.

Lawrence Sterne wrote of the Medmenhamites as 'a household of faith' and parodied the 'Benediction of Saint Paul', as he referred to Whitehead's 'Epistle of Paul to the Mednamites'. Whether he was a member, or whether he obtained his information on the society from his friend, Stevenson, is uncertain. Some literary students profess to see proof of his membership in a sly reference to one of the secret passwords of the Medmenham society by an allusion to the motto over the Cave of Trophonius in *Tristam Shandy*. Admittedly this motto was carved on the reproduction of the cave in the Abbey gardens, but this ancient pagan legend was often quoted in the eighteenth and early nineteenth centuries. Oddly enough, de Quincey in his *Confessions of an English Opium Eater* refers to it, and Rachel Antonina, Dashwood's illegitimate daughter, stayed with the de Quincey family at one period.

William Douglas, Earl of March, that vicious rake known as 'Old Q', was rumoured to have been one of the Brothers, but he seems only to have visited Medmenham on a few occasions. Nicholas Revett, fellow member of Dashwood in the Dilettanti Club, undertook much of the renovation of Medmenham Abbey at Dashwood's request, and, as the two men were friends, it is reasonable to assume that he too was a Franciscan. Revett was also responsible for the West Wycombe portico, called the Temple of Bacchus, completed in 1771.

The suggestion that Benjamin Franklin was a Brother has been received with loud noises of outraged indignation in some circles. Intensive research by various American University professors was carried out some years ago without their reaching any firm conclusion on the subject. Yet the probability is that Franklin was prevailed upon to join the society, even though he may not have taken part in all the proceedings. If Franklin joined, however, it must have been long past the heyday of the club and in a period when not only had the membership dwindled to a mere handful of Francis's cronies, but when the society had lost some of the zest which its Roaring Boy spirit of the early days engendered.

Franklin's early background encouraged rather than precludes the belief that he could have been a member. Though of Presbyterian stock, he was strongly anti-clerical in his young manhood and even expressed some outrageously worded attacks on Philadelphian clerics. In 1745 he spent a whole year of bawdy revelry in the taverns of Philadelphia, drinking rum and Madeira and even writing such verse as:

'Fair Venus calls; her voice obey;
In beauty's arms spend night and day.
The joys of love all joys excel
And loving's certainly doing well.'

This was very much in the Franciscan strain; at least it would explain why he not only tolerated but enjoyed the company of 'Saint' Francis. He was a frequent visitor to West Wycombe House and had ready access to his host's library, which he acknowledged in his correspondence. Van Doren, his most recent biographer, states that Franklin stayed at West Wycombe House in the summers of 1773 and 1774 and even more significantly refers to a sixteen-day visit there in July 1772. It was in June–July that Chapters of the Brotherhood were held and they normally lasted about two weeks. But we will re-examine Franklin's associations with West Wycombe in a later chapter, for his correspondence revealed that he knew of the existence of the caves.

Curiously, the story of how Dashwood came to know Franklin is an interesting little sidelight on one of his few sagacious acts as Chancellor of the Exchequer. However unfitted Dashwood may have been for this office, he was not only anxious to learn, but – further evidence of his submerged radical self – he wanted to reform the whole structure of British finance. Believing that he might get some progressive ideas from the administrators in the American colonies, he wrote to William Denny, a fellow member of the Royal Society and a former Governor of Pennsylvania, asking him for books on government finances in the colonies.

Denny gave him an introduction to Franklin and this was the beginning of a long and firm friendship. Incidentally, Dashwood had made a draft of various proposed reforms such as clarification of fees and legislation designed to eliminate petty graft. But it was not to be: his disastrous budget ended all that, drawing from the spiteful Walpole the comment: 'He performed so awkwardly, with so little intelligence of clearness, in so vulgar a tone.'

It says much for Dashwood's loyalty that (as Lord le Despencer) he braved the antagonism of both colleagues and friends to Franklin. Hillsborough, his joint-Postmaster General, did not get on well with Franklin, but le Despencer insisted on bringing them together and patching up any quarrels. Sandwich also hated Franklin, while Lord North refused to speak to him. When Franklin had to appear before the Privy Council in 1774, and Wedderburn launched a vitriolic attack on his character, le Despencer alone stood by him.

In an appendix at the end of this book is a list of those 'Monks' whose membership has been clearly established by several sources. To it is added a further list of those who, in the author's opinion, were probably members, but whose *bona fides* are confirmed by too few sources. Included in the latter list are the names of Frederick, Prince of Wales, and his one-time physician, Dr. Thomas Thompson. The only authority which can be quoted for the former is the *Dictionary of National Bibliography*, though it is believed that eighteenth-century papers of the Selby Lowndes family of Buckinghamshire may contain confirmation of this. As for Dr. Thompson, his bust was placed in the Mausoleum, but there is nothing else beyond his close friendship with Whitehead and Dodington to suggest he was a member.

There is, however, a third list of 'doubtfuls' and 'possibles'. In this list Horace Walpole is included, not as a serious possibility, but because, on the strength of the evidence quoted in previous chapters, his detailed knowledge of the Medmenhamites makes it impossible to rule him out entirely. If he were a member, it must have been a deliberate move on his part to spy on the society. It should also be noted that, though an enemy of le Despencer, he was on sufficiently good terms with him to present the Squire of West Wycombe with two flanking urns for the chimney piece of his house.

Another 'doubtful' member was the Rev. Timothy Shaw, who, according to various sources, was a Brother who drowned himself in the Thames in 1761 'to atone for his sinful ways'. This is entirely inaccurate. Shaw succeeded Edmund Duffield as Vicar of Medmenham and, according to the parish records, resigned in 1759, no reasons for this having been given. Lipscomb[1] testified that he afterwards became Vicar of Bierton. He almost certainly did not die in 1761, and it seems probable that the story of his drowning himself in the Thames is the result of his having been confused with Edmund Duffield.

Thomas Langley made some hand-written notes in the margin of his personal copy of *The Hundred of Desborough*[2] about various persons living in Medmenham in 1748–49. He mentioned 'an old bachelor and gentleman, Henry Edmund Stevens . . . a man of very few good, but a great many bad qualities, a miser, atheist, slanderer, whoremaster and interloper into other men's houses. Has been in France and Italy. Between fifty to sixty years old.' Stevens may very well have been one of the Brothers.

Another 'doubtful' is Henry Vanhattan, whose name appears in two lists of members. This may have been a mistaken reference to Henry Vansittart, and in preparing the lists the right and wrong spellings could both have been included.

Also mentioned in the author's final list are Giovanni Borgnis, son of Giuseppe, John Duffield, brother of Francis, Sir Joseph Banks, president of the Royal Society, W. Salamander and the Honourable Jack Spencer, kinsman of the Duchess of Marlborough.

Perhaps one of the strangest characters to figure in the list of 'doubtfuls' is that of the Chevalier d'Eon de Beaumont

1. *History of Buckinghamshire.*
2. Now in the Library of the Society of Antiquaries in Burlington House.

(1728–1810). Born in Burgundy, the sex of this extra-ordinary person seems to have been in doubt from the day of his birth. Though baptized as a boy, he was given the name of Genevieve as well as Charles, and was put in girl's clothes when three years old. Later he was dedicated to the Virgin Mary under the name of Charlotte. Sexual un-orthodoxy in any form has from the earliest times been accepted as a desirable qualification for intelligence work, and the freemasonry of such abnormal types was as marked in the eighteenth as in this twentieth century. In 1755 the Chevalier was sent to St. Petersburg as a secret agent, resuming women's clothes after having completed a military education. In fact he was received by the Empress of Russia as a woman and was described as her *letrice*.

He remained in Russia until 1760. Two years later he turned up in England as envoy to the Duc de Nivernais in connexion with the negotiations for the Treaty of Paris. He liked England, but seems to have got into trouble with the French authorities for refusing to put on woman's clothes again as instructed. He made friends with many of the Brothers, especially those who lived in Buckinghamshire, and he may have attended some of the gatherings in the caves, if not at Medmenham Abbey.

His only established visit to the Abbey had nothing to do with the society. This was on 24 May, 1771, when he was examined there by a jury of aristocratic ladies in order that judgment might be pronounced on his sex. The ladies after 'a most thorough investigation' returned a verdict of 'doubt-ful', a finding that by no means pleased those who had placed bets amounting to more than £100,000 in the hope of obtaining a positive decision one way or the other. Six years later these bets resulted in a lawsuit and a new jury found that he was a female, after which the Chevalier spent the remainder of his days dressed as such. When he died a doctor ruled with equal emphasis that he was 'without any shadow of doubt a male person' and he was buried as a male at St. Pancras.

The Chevalier was an eccentric person, but, though his name appears in two lists of possible members, there is no proof that he was one of the Friars. He is worth mentioning only for the reason that he alone of the Brothers (if he indeed were one) might be suspected of any sexual deviation. In fact, beyond the question mark attached to his sex, there is not even a fragment of gossip which might support a charge of abnormal sexual behaviour.

As has been seen, the most striking characteristic of the Medmenhamites was their antipathy to the Roman Catholic religion, a factor which would probably rule out the Chevalier as a member, though, as a secret agent of France, he might have had a dispensation to join. While in the persons of Sandwich, Potter, Whitehead and Wilkes this aversion to Catholicism extended to active atheism and blasphemy, among the majority of the members there was little more than a ribald agnosticism in their make-up. Quite a few, apart from Dashwood, supported the Church of England; even Churchill did not resign his curacy at St. John's, Westminster, until January, 1763. So his attacks on the Brotherhood were not launched because, as a clergyman, he had qualms about what went on at Medmenham, but solely for political reasons and, what is more, *immediately after* he left the Church.

Again, it cannot be over-emphasized that in none of the careers of the men mentioned in this chapter was there any evidence or hint of the practice of black magic or satanism other than the legends attaching to Sandwich. Even in his case the stories suggest practical joking rather than anything else.

Enemies of Rachel Antonina, le Despencer's illegitimate daughter, tried to revive the satanic legends of Medmenham by claiming that her father left her all his books of black magic, including a copy of *The Occult Philosophy*. This proves nothing and I prefer Rachel Antonina's own notes on her father's character: 'From an early association with the wits and *beaux esprits* of the fascinating age in which he lived my father delighted in *burlesque* pictures of life.'

The Medmenhamites must be judged by the standards of their age. Few of them were more promiscuous than Boswell, who was always succumbing to temptation in dark alleys with the dregs of humanity; most of them were more discriminating than Johnson's biographer and certainly far less hypocritical. But if this was a sensual age, it was also an age of intellectual rebellion, of fearless free-thinking, of self-criticism and soul-searching. Blasphemy was sometimes part of this revolt against centuries of superstition and, as youth mellowed into middle age, as often as not the sentiments that had seemed so bold and fashionable a decade before gave place to tolerance and moderation.

CHAPTER 7

GARDENS OF SCANDAL

THERE is nothing particularly erotic today either in the
gardens of Medmenham Abbey, or those of West Wycombe
Park, some six miles distant across the Chilterns. Elegance
and classical simplicity are the key-note to West Wycombe's
superb example of successful landscape gardening. But if
the eroticism and atmosphere of Bacchanalianism introduced by Dashwood and his colleagues have disappeared,
it is not surprising. For as early as 1800 Humphrey Repton
was called in to make 'judicious alterations' to the grounds,
and one need hardly doubt that he was unambiguously
instructed to remove all traces of the licentious imagery
which Wilkes and others have described.

Repton respected the general scheme of his predecessors,
and in his *Theory and Practice of Landscape Gardening*, published in 1803, he was generous enough to praise much of
the original work. He, too, was impressed, as were Langley
and Franklin, by the remarkable texture of the water '. . .
the brilliance of its colour, the variety of its shores, the
different courses of its channel, and the number of its
wooded islands, (it) possessed a degree of pleasing intricacy
which I have rarely seen in artificial pools or rivers'.

But before Repton's time the elements of decay had appeared. Bacchanalianism had become overgrown with
weeds and neglected Cupids looked scarred, chipped and
fretful. Thomas Langley, gazing sadly at the gardens only
three years before Repton started his alterations, said: 'Time
had spread its changing influence over these scenes, and by
adding wildness to the luxuriance of the vegetation, had
cast a gloom over the whole; on the house . . . depressing
the water, by darkening its surface, and on the lawn by
lengthened shadows.'

The gardens of Medmenham deteriorated even more

rapidly as the Franciscans' gatherings at the Abbey declined in number. Yet, in the late 'fifties, they were 'the gayest, the naughtiest, the most scandalous gardens to be found in all the length and breadth of the land'. Here, years afterwards, when gaiety had long since disappeared, Percy Bysshe Shelley wrote much of his verse on an island overlooking the Abbey.

But, though all traces of the Brotherhood have disappeared from Medmenham today, it is possible to recreate a factual, if perhaps somewhat embellished picture of those midsummer nights when the moon hung like a glowing opal in the violet sky above the gaunt old Abbey. . . .

Plashing gently and lazily through the otherwise still waters of the Thames, a scarlet gondola, like some painted swan, edged its way towards the banks of the Medmenham Abbey gardens. As the oarsmen relaxed, allowing the craft to glide leisurely with the current, their passenger read the following letter:

'Next Monday we meet at Medmenham. Pray remember the Ghost for me tonight.'

The letter was dated 15 June, 1762, and it was signed by John Wilkes.

Charles Churchill, the passenger and recipient of the letter, smiled to himself. The allusion to 'the Ghost' concerned a poem that the young poet was at that time writing. Or rather he was wrestling with the theme, for the poem, the subject of much conversation between the two, wouldn't work out to Charles's satisfaction. It was not surprising that he smiled rather wanly.

However, that night he decided that he would put the poem out of his mind and instead looked forward with pleasure to the prospect of wining with the 'Monks'. As the gondola nuzzled against the bank and nestled alongside a short buttress of stone which served as a pier, the young poet pushed the letter into his pocket and stepped ashore.

As the gondola swept away down the Thames a figure in a

long white cloak appeared from under the shadow of the elms.

'You are late,' he called across to the poet. 'What holds you back? Are you such a laggard to the call of Venus that you can waste so many precious minutes of Satan's blessed darkness?'

'Hello, there, Archbishop of Aylesbury! I have dallied in order to savour Venus's charms all the more. See, there she is – a lissom, glowing wench in the sky, warming our bellies, and lightening our hearts. . . .'

'You are not too drunk to have forgotten the password, I trust?' inquired the other.

'*Fay ce que voudras.*'

'So be it. Each man as he pleases until the Devil please otherwise. And the Devil is usually a Tory, or so it would seem.'

The two men went off together into the elms, through which the liquid beams of moonlight revealed the handsome but dissipated face of the man whom George III had called 'that Devil Wilkes' – John Wilkes, M.P. for Aylesbury, officer in the Bucks Militia, mob orator, rake and – to the Monks of Medmenham – 'Archbishop of Aylesbury'.

'Do the Tories still outnumber the Whigs at Medmenham?'

'Aye, they multiply every month. The Devil sees to that. The Devil and Paul the Aged.'

'That unspeakable Jacobite –'

'Yes, in a sense he is that. Purely for romantic reasons. And only because the Jacobites aren't ruling. Paul is a thorough-going Republican really. But he has had the misfortune to pimp with his pen for the Tories. A pity, for he has a nice turn of wit.'

'An arid wit.'

'Perhaps, and yet – Last night he said something rather good. Let me see, how did he put it? Oh, yes, he said the Brotherhood was a democracy where Bacchus was the King and every man better than his neighbour. I liked that.'

As the two men walked through the woods and on through the cunningly concealed groves and arbours towards the Abbey they paused occasionally to study an inscription on a leering faun, or a miniature nymph carved in stone.

'See how these woods echo our loves and frailties,' sighed Wilkes. 'Read this – ICI PAMA DE JOIE DES MORTELS LE PLUS HEUREUX. But round the corner is another of "Saint" Francis's frolics in stone. I call it a perpetual reminder to old George Bubb that, if he goes on as he has begun since the Monks came here, he will die in harness to some woman who can stay the pace better than a paunchy, wheezing old sexuagenarian.'[1]

They came to the 'reminder' in another corner, and Wilkes copied the inscription into a note-book. Shortly afterwards he published an account of these gardens in *The New Foundling Hospital for Wits*. Each one of the statues they saw that night he mentioned in detail in an article in this periodical. The 'reminder' to Bubb Dodington read: MOURUT UN AMANT SUR LE SEIN DE SA DAME.

They passed on. Carved on a fine old oak tree was the legend: HIC SATYRUM NAIAS VICTOREM VICTA FUGEBIT. In every nook, in every artificial cave, each inviting grotto there were messages, if not of open incitement to worship Venus, at least hints as to how others had availed themselves of the seclusion offered in these gardens. In one alcove they were greeted by this sensually inflammatory message: EN CET ENDROIT MILLE BAISERS DE FLAMME FURENT DONNES ET MILLE AUTRES RENDUS.

'Saint Francis thinks of everything. He mostly borrows from Virgil or Ovid, of course. Who better? But occasionally he tries his hand at composition, a Latin peculiarly his own. Hall Stevenson calls it Mackaroni Latin. See here, in this cave, carved over that mossy couch. Its meaning is clear enough – ITE AGITE, O JUVENES . . . I won't bore you by going on. That is Latin of a terseness which neither Caesar, nor His Majesty's Navy could equal in their signals.'

It was all rather childish, perhaps – certainly more like the sixth form composing smutty lyrics in Latin than the conduct of much-travelled men of the world and Members

1. Within six weeks of this date Dodington had died.

of Parliament. But then Dashwood himself was a satyr-like Peter Pan, who disliked growing up, and who, once the day's duties were done, revelled in these schoolboy pranks. Wilkes, though he had a pornographic mind, was much more mature than the average Franciscan. He had, too, an intensely critical mind and wide knowledge of the classics, and must have been more amused than enchanted with the tautology of lavatory wall Latin.

He was, however, particularly attracted by a statue of Venus stooping to pick a thorn from her foot. This statue was placed in the entrance to a grotto in such a position that any intruder would unexpectedly bump into the hind-part of the nude Goddess of Love. Just in case the full significance of this jest might be missed by the more obtuse, Wilkes recorded in *The New Foundling Hospital for Wits* that '. . . . just over the two nether hills of snow were these lines from Virgil:

> HIC LOCUS EST, PARTES UBI SE VIA
> FINDIT IN AMBAS: HAC ITER ELYZIUM NOBIS.
> AT LAEVA MALERUM EXERCET POENAS, ET AD
> IMPIA TARTARA MITTIT.'

There were innumerable grottoes containing grotesque statues with various attempts at puns in Latin in the inscriptions. Referring to one of these Wilkes wrote: 'The favourite doctrine of the Abbey is certainly not *penitence*, for in the centre of the orchard was a grotesque figure . . . and you might trace out:

> PENI TENTO
> NON
> PENITENTI

On the pedestal was a whimsical representation of Trophonius's Cave from whence all creatures were said to come out melancholy (*sic*). Among that strange, dismal group, you might however remark a cock crowing and a Carmelite laughing. The words GALLUM GALLINACEUM ET SACERDOTEM GRATIS were legible.'

By now the two friends were approaching the Abbey.

'And now for the revels,' said Wilkes. 'But first tell me how your new poem is going.'

'*The Ghost?*' inquired Churchill. 'It is still worrying me. I have worked on it for months and nothing happens, and perhaps it will be years before I finish it.'

'I think it is our own sweet Ghost who worries you most – our own little Sister Agnes.'

'I don't deny that I think a lot about her. Even in Tunbridge Wells – '

'Even there with my beloved little whore, Effie, to comfort you. Charles, you are becoming virtuous; you are forgetting the wise pagan scriptures.'

'It isn't only Sister Agnes, John, it is this whole hot-bed of intrigue and mystery. You laugh at it, you don't let it turn your head. You just make notes of what you see and keep a detached mind. But I can't forget that here in this temple of make-believe there is a pure child.'

'I shouldn't worry about Sister Agnes, Charles. She can look after herself. In any case she has Saint Francis for protector. He won't let her come to harm.'

'How can you believe that, knowing him for the cursed Tory that he is?'

'Oh, come, come, Charles. After all we are members of the same club and we are – or at least we ought to be – reasonable, civilized beings. Politics is one thing, but the good life is something to be shared, whether with Whig or Tory. I am a Republican, and so at heart are Dashwood and Whitehead. Sandwich, Dodington – they are the men I detest, and above all the brutish Bute, the Scots banzie with his false heart.'

'Of course, you are prejudiced. Dashwood is your fellow officer. But can you be so sure about his good nature? What about those tales John Hall Stevenson told about him?'

'Well, Stevenson is rather like you, Charles, a bigoted, bad-tempered Whig. I am a Whig, but I do not believe in letting it upset my liver or my love life. Act with the Whigs and whore with the Tories, I say. But, to do you justice, Charles, Stevenson is like his club – a Demoniac. If he had your freedom from malice, it would do him a lot of good.

But he indulges in what I call Whiggery-pokery. If he can't find a Jacobite under his bed, he dam' well invents one. I do not accept his tirades against Saint Francis. He would have us believe that Francis is an incestuous monster. Yet, when a few weeks ago I wrote to him and demanded proof, he declined and whiningly asked me to give "your absolution for my transgressions to Saint Francis". Now what do you think he meant by that?'

'It is obscure, like his verse, except when that verse is plain pornography, when it is so lucid as to be obscene.'

'Well, I do not think we shall see him at Medmenham again. I hardly think he would dare to put in an appearance. In any case most of our new members are Tories and aristocratic whoremongers like that repulsive old humbug, the Earl of March. I'm told that March has a spyhole specially built in his London house from which he ogles every woman passing by and makes indecent gestures to them.'

'Here is the Abbey. Let us go in.'

On summer evenings, when the breeze had dropped and it was too hot ashore, the Brothers used to go out on the river, some in small rowing boats, accompanied by laughing wenches in nuns' habits, and other larger parties in the scarlet gondola on one or other of the islands dotted about the Thames.

Wilkes talked enthusiastically about the Monks having 'a handsome pleasure boat' and Borgnis is supposed to have imported a gondola from Venice. The sight of the robed Monks and their masked women ensconced in a gondola, gliding across the Thames while they sang their bawdy catches must have provided a wonderful opportunity for the local Peeping Toms.

This was such a night. But some of the other Brothers had made the six miles journey to West Wycombe to boat on the lake. One must use considerable imagination to glean any idea of the eroticism these gardens evoked. Contemporary descriptions do not help much, nor is any plan of the Dash-wood lay-out known to be in existence. But from the mixture of facts and legends which has come down to us, aided by the four engravings of the gardens by William Woollett and a painting which hangs in the estate office at West Wycombe an approximate reconstruction is possible. Perhaps the best contemporary account is that of Arthur Young, the horticulturist, who gave this impression of the park, as he saw it in 1767: 'The situation is very agreeable on an eminence rising from a most elegant river, which meanders through the park and gardens, with the happiest effect; before the house it forms an elbow, which looks like a large lake, and on which floats a ship, completely rigged, with a long-boat, and another lying alongside; her masts rising above the adjoining trees in a manner which adds greatly to the landscape.'

Note the phrase 'an elbow'. This may or may not have been used accidentally, but it is reputed that one part of the park was laid out in the shape of a naked female. How this could have been fully appreciated in an age when there were no helicopters is not clear. Perhaps the lack of facilities for aerial observation enabled Dashwood to keep this a secret to his closest friends. Or perhaps when he built the Golden Ball on West Wycombe Church it was with the idea of surprising his friends with a glimpse of this spectacle. Pillars, artificial knolls, streams, thickets and other artifices are believed to have been introduced to give reality to this idea. Possibly, just as today trippers picnic on the eyes of various white horses on the South Downs, so the Monks had assignments with their 'Nuns' on various carefully selected parts of this horticultural Venus's anatomy.

There were temples and statues everywhere, rustic bridges and piers. The painting in the estate office shows a rotund temple on a small knoll around which are a cluster of statues with waving arms – a cavalcade of statues ranging down to the water's edge, where the scarlet gondola already mentioned is under way. An attempt had even been made to give the gondola its proper setting – an ornamental canal.

It was from this canal that some of the other Brothers were departing on this night, eagerly making their way to the stables where horses had been groomed ready to carry them to Medmenham. As usual, George Selwyn was the life and soul of the party.

'How does your new horse answer, George?' asked the rakish Sandwich.

'I really don't know, dear fellow,' drawled George. 'I have never asked him the question.'

'I hear that tedious painter Joshua Reynolds is to stand for Parliament,' chimed in another of the party.

'Yes, at Plympton, I believe. But do not laugh so soon. He may very well be elected, for Sir Joshua is the ablest man I know on a canvas.'

'Seen any executions lately, George?'

'Not for three weeks unless you count the removal of one of my teeth two weeks ago. Needless to say, that was regarded by Horace Walpole as a sign of my essential decadence. Horace happened to meet me leaving the dentist, and he promptly tells his friends: "George never thinks but *à la tête tranchée*. He came to town the other day and told the dentist he would drop his handkerchief for the signal to draw."'

There were hoots of merriment at this joke against himself. But George was launched on his favourite subject and not to be deterred from pursuing it.

'Hall Stevenson formed a regiment to find non-existent Jacobites in Yorkshire, but I did better than that. I went to see Lord Lovat fall to the axe. And then, for good measure, I made sure that this barbarism was avenged, for I waited to see them sew the head to its body again.

'Some men, like Potter, go to executions secretly and disguise themselves as old washerwomen – perhaps to excuse their squeamishness when they go green at the sight of blood. But not I. Everyone knows when I grace these salutary blood-lettings with my presence. Not long ago there was a man named Charles James Fox hanged at Tyburn. Needless to say the one and only Charles asked me if I had been to the execution.

"Not I," I replied. "I make a point of never attending rehearsals."'

The party mounted their horses and rode slowly off into

the woods. As they cantered along a strange and grotesque temple was outlined against the moon.

'Praise be to Saint Francis's monument to virility,' shouted Sandwich.

'The sight of such a column on a dark night would make even Lucy Cooper run screaming all the way from here to Drury Lane,' drily commented Selwyn. 'I suggest the nuns be made to parade past it every full moon.'

'For penitence?' inquired Sandwich.

'No. For *peni tento*.'[1]

Inside the Abbey was a subdued hush. Crimson lights burnt in corners of the long room, but they threw out only the faintest glow and in the alcoves leading to the cells all was darkness. This was the 'withdrawing room' and the only furniture was sofas covered with green silk damask.

Two remarkable and sinister statues were bathed in the crimson glow from concealed lights – on the one side the Egyptian Her-pe-Khred Horus, last born of Osiris, his finger to his lips, on the other the Volupian Angerona signalling back the same bequest for silence. For the Brothers this was a constant reminder of the need for secrecy.

Singly, in pairs and once in a party of four, the Brothers, garbed in their white hoods, entered the room. Presently the thick damask curtains on one side of the room were drawn back and there, resplendent in his red Cardinal's hat, stood 'Saint' Francis, and beside him, in mock solemnity, the Abbot of the Day, Paul Whitehead. It was the Abbot's duty to order the meals, fix the programme and generally act the role of master of ceremonies.

1. This temple must have been one of the most curious in the gardens. Many have referred to it as an atrocious piece of pornography, yet the most detailed description by Wilkes in *The New Foundling Hospital for Wits* is obscure. 'As to the temple,' he wrote, 'you find at first what is called an error *in limine* for the entrance to it is the same entrance by which we all come into the world and the door is what some idle wits have called the door of life. It is reported that on a late visit to his Chancellor Lord Bute particularly admired this building and advised the noble owner to lay out the £500 bequeathed to him in Lord Melcome's will for an erection in a Paphian column to stand at the entrance ... in Scots pebbles.'

'What is our command this night of our New Chapter?' intoned Whitehead.

'*Fay ce que voudras!*' shouted some twenty voices.

'Before we retire to receive our new Brother the Prior wishes to offer a libation to the Goddess without Eyes.'

'Saint' Francis then took a flagon of wine and poured out into wineglasses shaped like horns the ritual toast with which all Chapters commenced. It has been recorded that these glasses were a gift to the club by John Wilkes, who ordered them specially from Hemings to a design of his own. Five years later they were still unpaid for.

The toast having been drunk, a gong was sounded by Whitehead, and then in solemn file some of the Monks passed on into another room. In the darkness it was impossible to see whether Wilkes or Churchill followed them. The silence in the withdrawing room was broken only by the slow, monotonous intonations of Whitehead and the rumble of an occasional response. Whether they were 'prayers to His Satanic Majesty', as Johnston averred, is extremely doubtful. One heard the words *Bona Dea* and *Maia*, suggesting fertility rites rather than mock Satanism. Then at the end came the ringing tones of 'Saint' Francis's virile voice proclaiming: 'Henceforth, Brother — I name thee of the company of Saint Francis.'

And with the inevitable cry of *Fay ce que voudras* the proceedings came to an end and the Monks filed out again.

As they entered the withdrawing room Whitehead paused a moment to carry a lighted taper to two lamps at either end of the chamber. Now the faces of the Monks could be clearly distinguished; Sandwich, saturnine and sinister in his fascinating ugliness; Selwyn, elegant and composed; Sir Thomas Stapleton, Wilkes and Churchill.

The reason for the additional light was soon evident. Drawn up in a long line on one side of the room were hooded 'Nuns', only the black masks on their faces suggesting anything that was not ecclesiastical in their appearance. There they stood, silent, demure and watchful, for this was the identification procession by which each 'Nun' made sure that no Brother was present whom she did not wish to see.

It was a wise precaution, decreed by 'Saint' Francis, and, for an age not particularly noted for its chivalry, revealed a charming gallantry on the part of the 'Father of the Order'. For while the amours of the women remained carefully hidden, when they so desired it, male members could conceal none of their designs from the 'Nuns'.

Solemnly the Brothers filed past the ladies, who coquettishly fanned themselves and then, at a signal from Whitehead, the lines of Monks and Nuns broke up and intermingled. Chatter, laughter and greetings filled the chamber. Males and females retired in pairs, while others stood around in groups. A servant brought in a tray of drinks. From somewhere then in the background came the sound of violins.

Not all the Brothers pursued the 'Nuns'. Wilkes went into the Abbey library where Selwyn and Stapleton were about to begin a game of backgammon.

'What brings you here, Archbishop?' inquired Stapleton. 'Have you come for quiet meditation?'

'I've come to see the Franciscan editions of the Prayer Book,' replied Wilkes, taking down a book from the shelves. 'Or perhaps I should say the Curll edition.'

'Oh, Saint Francis has a better printer than Master Curll. You should read the *Ave Maria* of Master Coustance, a gem of pagan ritual as practised by the black magicians of Venice.'

'Tell me, Brother Thomas, is that the book on which our faith was founded when Paul the Aged and Saint Francis used to meet at the George and Vulture?'

'My dear Archbishop, Saint Francis requires little more than his own satanic inspiration in these matters. But he did consider this work to be an admirable, even a serious answer to the brouhaha of Rome.'

'An aperient for prurient bowels,' smirked Selwyn. 'An antidote for chaplains who might be better employed preparing the sentenced man for hell rather than heaven. And, forsooth, an aphrodisiac to breathe fire into the belly of an over-virtuous maiden.'

The two men continued with their game and Wilkes went on examining the books. There were rows of them, black-bound heavy tomes with sanctimonious titles, which, on being opened, disclosed the salacious works of Edmund Curll, pornographic novels and poems which never found their way on to the open market. A year afterwards, when Walpole visited the library, he found 'scurrilous novels bound as Books of Common Prayer'.

In another room Sandwich was dandling a 'Nun' on his knee. Despite his protests she refused to remove her mask and rapped his fingers when he tried to pull it off.

'No, no, you must make three guesses ere I take it off,' she laughed.

'The voice I know, but the eyes deceive me. Elizabeth Roach?'[1]

'No.'

'Frances Vane?'

'You flatter me.'

'Then, by Angerona herself, it can only be the one and only Betty Weyms.'

The 'Nun' snapped her fan and tossed her head. 'You go from the sublime of Lady Vane to the ridiculous of Mistress Hayes's salons, sir. Do my eyes so deceive you that you believe one to be the glass eye of Betty Weyms?'[2]

'If it be not glass, then it is some devilish oriental trick to make it glisten.'

'It is kohl, sir. I should have thought after your experience of Turkish harems, you would have known of its qualities.'

'Do not trifle with me any longer,' said Sandwich, now angry. 'Declare yourself.'

'There is no rule of this Order which forces me to do so. There is nothing to prevent me from withdrawing this instant, masked if I wish.'

1. Elizabeth Roach was said to be one of Dashwood's mistresses.
2. Betty Weyms was a close associate of the notorious bordello keeper, Charlotte Hayes; she had a glass eye which she was always losing on her visits to the Rose Tavern.

'*Fay ce que voudras*. You do as you please – remain masked if you will. And I will do as I please and whisk you off to my cell.'

Without further ado Sandwich picked up the unprotesting wench and carried her off into one of the alcoves.

Meanwhile Charles Churchill, suffering from claustrophobia in the stuffy confines of the Abbey and the oppressiveness of damask curtains, had gone for a stroll in the gardens with one of the 'Nuns'. She was a pert, flaxenhaired minx imported to the Abbey for a few days from Charlotte Hayes's establishment.

'Why must you walk all this way, Brother Charles, when the cell is so much more comfortable?'

'Comfortable and convenient it may be, but it distracts me to be within ear range of that monster Sandwich.'

'But where are you taking me? The Chapel of Ease, or the river? If it is the river, I hope you can manipulate a boat better than Brother John of Magdalen.'

'I want to ask you something that I wish no one else to hear. Can you tell me what has happened to Sister Agnes?'

'Sister Agnes or *Saint* Agnes, do you mean?'

'*Saint*, I agree, is what she should be called.'

'I haven't seen her during my last two visits to Medmenham.'

'Nor I. But do you know where she is?'

'Why are you so interested? It isn't very polite, Brother Charles, to take me into the woods just to talk about Saint Agnes.'

'I have brought you to the woods to find a better bed in Nature's moss than ere I shall find in those monkish cells. I do not talk about Saint Agnes for any other purpose than I am seriously anxious about her safety. I was told she would be here tonight.'

'Well, she isn't far away.'

'Where?'

'Sit down, Brother Charles, and I will tell you all I dare. But won't you kiss me first – just to show a little interest. I assure you Santa Carlotta would think little of my talents if she thought I amused you not one iota. Look at this brooch and read its motto, Charles – "Love and Friend-ship". Can't we live up to it?'

Together they sat down on the mossy bank not far from the cave dedicated to Trophonius. They made an odd pair – Charles Churchill, looking as full of melancholy as one of the creatures crawling from that mythical cave, and the minx from Charlotte Hayes's bagnio, a small, high-cheek-boned miss with a merry, coquettish mouth, trying to appear as coy and virginal as possible. The soft night air caressed them; masses of warm, enveloping shadows shrouded their mossy couch and the perfume of syringa provided a cosy, cloying background for an amorous interlude. But *l'amour* for once was not in Churchill's mind.

'What a lovely night! said the girl, tossing back her curls and nestling her head against Charles's shoulder. In the leaves luminous patches trembled; the trees seemed to give out a sultry sweetness; the duck-weeds shone like a green light on the river's edge and the frogs contributed a tremu-lous concerto of their own.

'The very night itself conspires to rouse one's blood. Don't you prefer this to the cribbed and confined cells of the Abbey?'

'I'm almost glad you brought me here after all. Without you, though, I'd be mightily scared in the dark. Can't you spare an arm to make me feel it's you and not the frogs I have for an escort?'

Somewhat ungallantly and impatiently Churchill slipped an arm round her. But his mind was elsewhere and she knew it. Irritated, she wiped the beads of dew from her curls and, pouting her pretty lips, petulantly inquired:

'Why can't you be nice to me, Charles?'

'Because I want an answer to my question.'

'And you promise if I give it, that you will tarry with me here a while?'

'If you give me the right answer, I'll ravish you to cock crow. Nothing will give me greater pleasure than to stay away from the Abbey.'

'Don't sound so fierce about it. You talk as though you would crush the life out of me.'

'I will if you don't tell me what I want to know. You'll be so bruised and crushed that Santa Carlotta will think you've been to Mistress Birch's Flagellation School in Chapel Street instead of with the Mackaronies of Medmenham.'

'Well, listen carefully, and I'll tell you. Agnes has been sent away at the command of "Saint" Francis. I do not know why, but I suspect that one of the "Lady Nuns" is having a baby and that Agnes is in charge of her. There may be more to it than that, for Sister Agnes has always been a mystery to us.'

'But where is she?'

'I don't know exactly, but I have a shrewd idea. You know that "Saint" Francis has built the new road from West Wycombe to High Wycombe. Well, to get the materials for this road, he had to dig deep into West Wycombe Hill. For a few years he has had labourers tunnelling into the hillside. And down in the village there are whispers that "Saint" Francis has turned these tunnels into caves.'

'Caves in the hillside? Whatever for?'

'You mustn't breathe a word about it. I should not be asked to Medmenham again, if it were thought that I had peached. Very few know about these caves – only the Superiors of the Order. I think they may occasionally meet there instead of in the Chapel.'

'And you mean to say you believe Agnes is in the caves, perhaps held there as a prisoner?'

'I cannot be sure. I don't say she is a prisoner. I am sure "Saint" Francis treats her quite well, but my guess is that she now lives in the caves.'

'Thank you,' replied Churchill. 'That is all I wanted to know. And now you shall have your reward for that information – in kisses, wine and moonlit rapture!'

CHAPTER 8

JOHN WILKES

In 1762 the formation of the ill-starred government of the Earl of Bute marked the beginning of dissension, quarrels and disintegration in the ranks of the Medmenhamites.

Shortly after Bute took office, Dashwood wrote to John Wilkes, saying: 'The deficiency in the law, the neglect and insolence of turnkeys, the unwearied misapplications of the colonels are matters of no wonderment to me, but I can tell you what will make you wonder, and that very justly, when you hear that His Majesty has been pleased to appoint me his Chancellor of the Exchequer.'

This letter suggests that, though political opponents, Dashwood and Wilkes were on the best of terms at this date. Note, too, that they would both appear to share certain critical views of administration generally. But apart from the evidence of this letter, there is the fact that Dashwood recommended and wholeheartedly endorsed the appointment of Wilkes as his successor as Colonel of the Bucks Militia.

These are important points to remember, for, throughout the dissensions of the next few years, despite unscrupulous political and personal attacks launched by one Medmenhamite against another, Dashwood and Wilkes not only continued to respect each other but even kept up a private friendship. Wilkes, it is true, scoffed at Dashwood's administration at the Treasury and sneered about his peerage as 'decorating his fall', but there was nothing malicious in any of his references to Dashwood.

John Wilkes was one of the most remarkable and underestimated men of his age. History has not been kind to him, and there is still a tendency to lay far too much stress on his licentious private life and too little on his political ability.

Raymond Postgate in his biography *That Devil Wilkes* wrote that he began 'in the usual belief that Wilkes was an amusing but entirely dishonest man'. After more than three years of study he was forced to change his opinion and believed that 'Wilkes was politically an honest man'.

The truth was that Wilkes was something new in Georgian times. He was the symbol of the rise of an articulate and educated middle class in a society dominated by the oligarchy of wealthy, much-travelled squires. While he was a tub-thumping democrat, the idol of the masses and a fiery rebel, he was also a widely read man with an outstanding knowledge of the classics. His talent in Latin and Greek was matched by very few of his contemporaries. Naturally he was resented by his political opponents, who, jealous of his intellect and ability, sought to denigrate him. But Dashwood never had any doubts as to his talent and accepted him as an equal, thoroughly enjoying his company.

Educated at Leyden University, Wilkes, the son of a distiller, rejected his Calvinist upbringing and became a confirmed agnostic. He made no secret of this and it was he who persuaded Charles Churchill to quit his curacy and 'put an end to this futile pretence'. Brougham, a prejudiced historian, said of him: 'If we are to judge of his speaking by the very few samples preserved of it, we should indeed form a very humble estimate of its merits. But what it wanted in force, it probably made up for in fury. All the people in London were hanging on the lips of their leader; yet nothing could be worse or feebler than his speech.'

This was an unfair judgment. In election campaigns he had a gift of repartee unrivalled in his day.

'Will you vote for me?' inquired Wilkes at one pre-election meeting.

'I'd sooner vote for the Devil,' shouted a surly opponent.

'But if your friend doesn't run, may I count on your support?'

He could always turn his wit as readily against himself as against others. When the King received him at a levee in later years when his popularity had waned, the former inquired after 'your friend, Sergeant Glyn.'

'Sir,' replied Wilkes, 'he is not a friend of mine. He was a Wilkite, which I never was.'

As Member of Parliament for Aylesbury he was launched into politics under the banner of the Temple-Pitt faction of the Whigs. Thomas Potter retired from the Aylesbury seat in order to let Wilkes in. It is believed that his introduction to Dashwood was made either by Lord Temple, or Thomas Potter, with whom he struck up a close friendship. Lord Temple of Stowe was his patron and recommended him to Dashwood as 'an ideal officer for your regiment'. He also owed his High Sheriffship of Buckinghamshire to Temple.

His matrimonial life was launched in the worst possible circumstances and may largely explain his unbridled lechery in later years. He married – against his better judgment and solely to please his parents – Mary Mead, a fat and ugly woman ten years older than he. They set up house together with Wilkes's mother-in-law, a possessive, dominating woman with a passion for religion. It was more than Wilkes could stomach and he made no pretence to mollify her. The wild parties and drinking bouts which took place at his house in Great George Street so shocked his mother-in-law that she more or less forced a separation of man and wife. It was after this separation that Wilkes became M.P. for Aylesbury.

Wilkes proved himself a competent officer in the Militia and soon won the warm regard of Dashwood. Round about 1758 he was enrolled as a member of the Brotherhood. He regarded the club as an excellent provider for his needs in women and wine and looked upon the mock rituals as a brilliant piece of practical joking. Before he launched his sly attacks on the Brotherhood, his correspondence reveals him to have been an enthusiastic member. On 15 June, 1762 (the same day that he wrote the letter to Churchill quoted in the last chapter) he wrote to Dashwood: 'I feast my mind with the Joys of Medmenham on Monday and hope to indemnify myself there for the noise and nonsense here.'[1]

But a regard for Dashwood did not prevent his developing

1. Egerton MSS. 2136, f. 47 (British Museum).

a contempt and hatred for some of the other Brothers. His particular enemies were Sandwich and Bubb Dodington, but probably the one incident which alienated him most from the Franciscans was the admission of Bute as a member. 'The damned Scotsman and his Government' was Wilkes's chief political target throughout 1762–63, and he was determined to use every weapon in his armoury of satire and irony to bring down the Prime Minister.

These two years brought to Wilkes a considerable amount of unfavourable publicity, much of which he courted deliberately. A lesser man would have been broken by the concentrated attacks made against him and the consequent damage done to his already dubious reputation in private life, but Wilkes had an amazing capacity for riding out political storms. During the whole of this period his daughter Polly, to whom he was sincerely and passionately devoted, seems to have been his chief consolation.

But it was not politics which precipitated the storm in the first place, or his final and fatal quarrel with Sandwich, but a typical Wilkesean jest. There are several versions of this, but the most detailed, though possibly also the most highly coloured, is that given by Johnston in *Chrysal*. According to Johnston someone who filled the 'office of keeper of the Chapel' at Medmenham dressed up a baboon in a black robe with horns on its head and hid it in a chest in the Chapel. It is confirmed by other sources that Wilkes was the man who did this, but it is very doubtful whether he held any such office as that mentioned by Johnston.

During one of the Chapters, when the Brothers were intoning their mock prayers, Wilkes, unnoticed in the dim light, opened the chest and freed the animal. Immediately it went berserk, chattering away in what must have seemed like a satanic gibberish, its horns shaking on its head. Something like terror descended on many of the Brothers and men who were rational enough in their everyday life and not prone to superstition were panicked into believing that some supernatural agent had come to admonish them. Shrieks rent the Chapel and these, together with the imbecile mutterings of the baboon, must have caused even more

135

consternation to any servants in other parts of the building.

Some Brothers dived to the ground and hid their faces from the sight of the 'fantastically garbed Devil'. But the 'Devil', having been pent up for so long in the chest, was revelling in his new-found freedom. He promptly jumped on Sandwich's back and clung there, screaming. According to Johnston, Sandwich fell to his knees and cried: 'Spare me, gracious Devil. I am as yet but half a sinner. I never have been so wicked as I pretended.'

Possibly to some extent Sandwich spoke truly, not only on behalf of himself, but of all the Monks. One may see in this unpremeditated statement by Sandwich a tacit admission that they had merely been playing at black magic and not genuinely practising Satanism.

The humiliation of Sandwich and some of the others when they discovered that the incident was a practical joke conceived by Wilkes must have been acute. By this single act he had laid bare the follies, latent superstitions and childishness of some of the members and dealt the puerile rituals of the club a mortal blow. Humiliation swiftly gave way to anger. 'The Society,' wrote Johnston, 'agreed on solemn oath that no member should ever after presume to attempt exercising his wit upon the society in any manner, or by any means whatsoever.'

Then Johnston made a statement which would seem to rule out the generally accepted theory that Churchill was the source of his information. For he added: 'My master thought that this was much too mild for so flagrant a crime.' If Churchill were his master, it is unlikely that he, the friend of Wilkes, took any such view. Thus, as has been previously suggested, it is possible that Johnston got the story from Lord Mount Edgecumbe, who heard it from Sandwich. In this case 'my master' may have referred to Sandwich or one of his friends.

Apparently the view that this was too mild a punishment prevailed, for Johnston recorded that 'They all took fire at the thought of their dignities being insulted and expelled him without hearing him in his own defence.'

The date of this incident cannot be fixed, though it is said that Wilkes was expelled from the Brotherhood in 1763. But it is not absolutely certain that any formal expulsion took place. Wilkes's marginalia in his own personal copy of *The History of the Late Ministry* states: 'It is perhaps singular with respect to this periodical (he was referring to *The North Briton*) that it was conducted upon principles different from any other. No private tie had been broke, no connexion dissolved, nor any attack begun where there was friendly intercourse. Sir Francis Dashwood will be on record a remarkable proof of this observation. He was certainly as Chancellor of the Exchequer the best mark an Opposition could wish. He was spared by *The North Briton* and it was believed he owed that indemnity to private connexions with Mr. Wilkes.

'He was one of the Monks of Medmenham and used to attend the Chapters very regularly. He afterwards neglected those meetings and gave us the reason that he did not choose to meet Mr. Wilkes who was an enemy of Lord Bute. Mr. Wilkes desir'd their common friends at the Abbey to represent to Sir Francis the nature of such an institution in which party had not the least concern.'

This statement does not suggest that Wilkes was expelled. But undoubtedly the prank with the baboon greatly strained the tolerance and good fellowship of the members and made Sandwich an implacable enemy of Wilkes. Whether Wilkes introduced the baboon to Medmenham, or whether it was already there is not clear. The probability is that this was the baboon presented to the Brothers by Henry Vansittart, Governor of Bengal, and that Wilkes came across it quite by chance and perpetrated this prank on the spur of the moment. If so, the baboon must have been an unfamiliar object to the Brothers, for, had it previously been dressed up as Satan and used in Black Mass ceremonies (as has been suggested), it is unlikely that it would have deceived the Brothers on this occasion.

Incidentally, W. Bolton in an article on 'The Medmenham Friars' in the *Ex Libris Journal* of April 1901 claimed that the baboon 'leapt on the shoulders of Lord Orford' (a nephew of Horace Walpole) and not on Sandwich. But it is likelier that the berserk animal leapt on several shoulders.

Johnston said that the servants caught sight of the black-robed and horned baboon during the fracas in the Chapel and that they spread the rumour that the Devil had visited Medmenham. 'After that,' he said, 'the monastery was closed.' This incident may have disrupted club activities for some time, but the society continued to function at Med-menham for several years afterwards. Nevertheless, it is probably true that the episode of the baboon, combined with political squabbles, led to the disintegration of the Brotherhood.

From Wilkes's marginalia one would gather that the club broke up into warring factions about this period. If Lord le Despencer did not attend the club gatherings, who presided in his stead? Or is it possible that some members still went to the Abbey, while others, led by Despencer, adjourned to the caves at West Wycombe?

Lord Bute founded a Government newspaper called *The Briton*, which was edited by Dr. Smollett. Wilkes immediately replied to this by launching *The North Briton*. The chicanery and corruption surrounding the Treaty of Paris in 1763 made the Bute Government extremely unpopular, and in No. 45 of *The North Briton* Wilkes referred to the King's congratulations on the Peace of Paris as 'an abandoned instance of ministerial effrontery'. The King was furious and lodged a complaint against the newspaper.

While the House of Commons was debating the King's complaint an incident occurred which is thus referred to by Horace Walpole in his letters to Mann: 'One Mr. Martin, who has much the same quarrel with Mr. Wilkes as King George, and who chose to suspend his resentment, like His Majesty, till with proper dignity he could notify his wrath to Parliament, did express his indignation with rather less temper than the King had done, calling Mr. Wilkes to his face "cowardly scoundrel". Mr. Wilkes inquired of Mr. Martin by letter next morning if he, Mr. Wilkes, was meant by him, Mr. Martin, under this periphrasis. Mr. Martin replied in the affirmative, and accompanied his answer with a challenge. They immediately went into Hyde Park, and, at the second fire, Mr. Wilkes received a bullet in his body.'

Wilkes was no coward and he fought a number of duels. After his duel with Lord Talbot in October 1762 he wrote: 'A sweet girl, whom I have sighed for unsuccessfully these four months now tells me she will trust her *honour* to a man who takes so much care of his own. Is that not prettily said?'

When Wilkes lay wounded after receiving the bullet from Martin, he believed himself to be dying, and he told his adversary: 'You are a man of honour. I am killed, so make good your escape.'

He even returned to Martin a letter from the latter which he had been carrying so that no evidence against Martin should be found on his (Wilkes's) body. Such precautions were unnecessary, for Wilkes soon recovered.

Meanwhile from the pens of Wilkes and Churchill came oblique attacks on the pro-Bute section of the Brotherhood. Wilkes's descriptions of the society at Medmenham Abbey appeared in print. It is true they were good-humoured satire rather than malicious assaults, but they constituted a breach of the code of secrecy which members had imposed upon themselves. Wilkes excused himself by pointing out that he had declined to reveal anything of the activities of the 'Inner Council' of the Brotherhood. But this may have been merely because Wilkes was not in the 'inner circle' and consequently knew nothing of what went on. In Wilkes's defence it might be argued that, if he had been expelled from the society, he was absolved from any pledge of secrecy.

Soon members of both factions were slanging one another. Hogarth called Wilkes a 'miscreant' and attacked Churchill for putting the gist of *The North Briton* onslaught into heroic verse. Churchill replied with his *Epistle to Hogarth*. The latter, infuriated, responded with a bitter caricature of Wilkes, to whom he gave a satanic grin, and a representation of Churchill as a bear with a staff, on which 'lie the first, lie the second, and lie the tenth' were engraved in unmistakable letters. 'I so patched up a print of Master Churchill,' wrote Hogarth, 'revealing him in the character of a bear; the pleasure and pecuniary advantage which I derived from these two engravings together with occasionally riding on horseback, restored me to as much health as I can expect at my time of life.'

It was by a subtle mixture of satire and sarcasm that Wilkes was most damaging to the Brotherhood. He made no personal attacks on Dashwood, who was almost the only member of the Bute faction to be spared from the vituperations of *The North Briton*. But in seemingly innocent descriptions of irrelevance he made mischief. Thus in *The New Foundling Hospital for Wits* Wilkes described West Wycombe House as containing 'nothing remarkable excepting only that there is on the grand staircase a very moral painting of a maid stealing to her master's bed, laying at the same time her finger on her lips as if she were the *Dea Angerona* of West Wycombe'.

And again he spoke of finding a gold button with the letters IHS and the Sign of the Cross engraved on it in the gardens of West Wycombe House. The implication was that this button was used by Sir Francis in some ritual.

It is almost impossible to assess whether Wilkes was out openly to expose the Brotherhood and lampoon them, or whether he just could not help poking fun at them and being impishly provocative. No doubt there was a mixture of both sentiments. Perhaps his success in outwriting the Government after the attack on No. 45 of *The North Briton* made him careless and uncaring. Both Wilkes and Kearsley, his printer, were arrested, and Wilkes was sent to the Tower of London and deprived of his colonelcy of the Militia. But the Ministers who had been so eager to destroy him forgot in their anger to make sure that their actions were within the law. The result was that Chief Justice Pratt ordered the release of Wilkes on the grounds of privilege of Parliament and the illegality of the warrants against him.

For a few weeks Wilkes was the hero of London, if not of the whole nation. Crowds cheered him all the way back home with a torchlight procession, improvised bands and fireworks. For the first, but not the last time the cry 'For Wilkes and Liberty' was heard.

In verse the general feeling was expressed:

'To what dirty tricks have some great ones descended
To ruin poor Wilkes, who our rights has defended.
But Britons be bold, they can ne'er gain their ends,
While Justice and Pratt are fair Liberty's friends.'

The battle of Wilkes against Bute and his Ministers was renewed, not only through those periodicals with which the former was most closely associated, but in other media, too. In the *Public Advertiser* on 22 January, 1763, there appeared a cartoon showing two Medmenham Monks with this caption:

'This day is published a new Ludicrasito called "Secrets of a Convent", etched by that droll novice, Pietro Apastino, and published by Matt Darly.'

In the *Public Advertiser* of May 1763 was the following:

'Some of the curious articles in the inventory you published have been imported from France (*by Wilkes*) . . . to complete the valuable collection of the sort (*referring to pornographic works*) which is in the saloon of the famous Convent on the banks of the Thames, called Medmenham Abbey, where the Right Hon. the Lord le Despencer presides with such decency and order and has spent many a jovial day with Mr. Wilkes before their late differences in politics.

'It is hoped his Lordship's interest will be able to procure a restitution of the goods to Mr. Wilkes, or a grant to the Abbey of the forfeiture upon Mr. Wilkes' conviction that the members of that noble institution may not be injured by the offence of a brother.'

It is difficult to find the right interpretation of this obscure appeal. Undoubtedly it referred obliquely to Wilkes's imprisonment, but whether this was a genuine appeal for a restitution of the books made by Wilkes himself, or whether it was written by someone on his behalf, or, again, by an enemy of Wilkes, it is impossible to say. Wilkes never denied his membership of the Brotherhood; in fact, he frequently admitted it and on some occasions even defended the club he had so often satirized.

Many people have sought to show that Wilkes was at the best an unreliable witness, at the worst an unmitigated liar. But as soon as one attempts to analyse these sweeping generalizations, they fall to the ground. No man has been more frequently misquoted or misrepresented than he, and in his testimony concerning the Brotherhood it is extremely difficult to fault him. Allowing for a considerable amount of political bias and anti-Tory propaganda, Wilkes's accounts of the club and its members are fairly well substantiated. On the whole there does not appear to have been any personal spleen in his articles on the Brotherhood, and both he and Churchill visited Lord le Despencer at West Wycombe in 1763, when they were taken to 'the magnificent gilt ball on the top of the steeple, which is hollowed and made so very convenient in the inside for the celebrations not of devotional, but of convivial rites'. That Wilkes could write in this fashion a year after he was supposed to be expelled from the club and drink 'divine milk punch' with le Despencer suggests that they were still on good terms in private if not in public. All the same he could not refrain from the impish comment that: 'I must own that I was afraid my descent from it (the globe) would have been as precipitate as his Lordship's was from a high station, *which turned his head, too.* I admire likewise the silence and secrecy which reign in the globe, undisturbed but by his jolly songs, very unfit for the profane ears of the world below.'

So there is the incredible enigma of the period. Wilkes slyly satirizing the Brothers in print, a vehement political opponent of le Despencer, alienated from at least half the club's members, yet happily drinking milk punch hundreds of feet above the ground with 'Saint' Francis and joining him in bawdy songs into the bargain. The prospect of two political opponents ensconced together in such an environment is one of those recurring phenomena which so baffle foreign students of British life.

'A nation's reckoning, like an alehouse score,
Whilst Paul the Aged chalks behind the door.'

By the 'nation's reckoning' Churchill was indicating the mounting public indignation at the revelations of what went on at Medmenham. The tittle-tattle in the newspapers and scandal sheets soon spread to the taprooms of the bourgeoisie. By the time the news had percolated to the illiterate masses the Society of 'Saint' Francis had been distorted beyond recognition. To the mob it was the 'Hell-Fire Club' come to life again, and they lapped up the rumours of satanism and Black Masses, becoming firmly convinced that the society was peopled by 'Jacobites, Tories, Roman Catholics and sodomites!' Such were the popular prejudices of the uneducated anti-Papists that they equated Jacobism, Catholicism and unnatural vice and saw no difference between the masses of Rome and those of Satan.

But it was not from Wilkes or Churchill that the final blow came, but from Sandwich. Wilkes had set up a printing press at his house in Great George Street and news of this had filtered through to Government circles. After the suppression of *The North Briton* as a seditious libel Wilkes was obviously intending to take greater precautions in future. But he acted too late; the Government, realizing that his former printers were probably not too pleased that they had lost his custom, set out to bribe them into providing further evidence of sedition. In this they failed; Kearsley was loyal to Wilkes and refused to accept any bribes.

From an unexpected quarter, however, came a sensation for which the Government were not looking and which, to be fair, embarrassed them. From a printer named Michael Curry, who had done some work privately for Wilkes, came a single copy of an indecent work entitled *Essay on Woman*. That copy came into the hands of a disreputable clergyman named Kidgell, who was Rector of Horne in Surrey and chaplain to that eccentric and dissolute rake, the Earl of March.

From Kidgell there is little doubt that the copy of *Essay on Woman* went to the Government. But before this step was taken Kidgell undoubtedly consulted his patron, the Earl of March. 'Old Q' passed the information on to Sandwich and incited Kidgell to write a pamphlet attacking the

Essay. In this he described the *Essay* as a work of outrageous blasphemy and an indecent parody of Pope's *Essay on Man*. Wilkes, at first merely amused, replied with a tracit satirizing the hypocritical Kidgell, himself the author of an obscene book, *The Card*, and a former member of a Hell-Fire Club at Oxford.

The more moderate members of the Government were not anxious to see a charge brought against Wilkes. This was not because they feared Wilkes as an adversary, but that they took the view that this was a private publication and, therefore, to some extent privileged. Few of them had not read the pornographic literature of the earlier part of the century, circulated by Curll and others, and it was generally known that Kidgell was a revolting specimen of the priesthood. The Lord Chancellor (Northington) was himself a jovial rake and he did not agree with the charge being made. But the right-wing Tories and a few Whigs were cock-a-hoop at the prospect of downing Wilkes and obliterating their ignominious defeat over the prosecution of *The North Briton*. Sandwich, seizing on his chance of revenge, gave one of the most nauseating speeches ever heard in the House of Lords. He denounced the Member for Aylesbury in tones of unctuous hypocrisy, expressing mock horror at the wickedness and appalling blasphemy of *The Essay*. Yet he himself was expelled from the Beefsteak Club for blasphemy and had always been the most virulent exponent of atheism among the Brothers. Those among his peers who knew Sandwich intimately tittered at this feigned display of outraged virtue and the more cynical afterwards complimented him on his 'new-found sense of propriety'.

Le Despencer, however, adamantly declined to join in the attack. He is said to have been deeply shocked by Sandwich's speech. The two men had always prided themselves on speaking out without fear or favour on what they believed or disbelieved, and le Despencer felt that Sandwich had surrendered this, his sole virtue – honesty. Turning to a fellow peer, le Despencer whispered: 'I never thought to live and hear Sandwich express such sentiments. This is undiluted sermonizing of the most repulsive kind. Never before have I heard the Devil himself preaching.'

But the hypocritical oratory of Sandwich forced the issue. Parliament had met on 15 November, 1763, and the Commons endorsed the verdict of the Lords. On 19 January, 1764, Wilkes was expelled from the House and on 21 February he was convicted on two charges of libel. Virtually outlawed, he lived in France and Italy until 1768, but was sufficiently the old Wilkes to find for himself in Paris a new mistress, named Corradini.

The only parallel to the *Essay on Woman* case in modern times was that of the diaries of Sir Roger Casement. It seems inevitable that at least once in every century British morality must unite with all the more raucous voices of immorality in raising some bogus scare of indecency. And just as the Casement affair remains unsolved, casting a nasty smear on British Justice, so that of the *Essay on Woman* still defies the efforts of historians, biographers and students of literature to unravel it.

There must be at least a score of versions of the *Essay* in existence, some of them palpable forgeries; in addition many writers have sought to explain and interpret them. The only point in dwelling on the controversy in this chapter is that the *Essay* was directly concerned with the Brotherhood of 'Saint' Francis. The question of whether Wilkes wrote it remains unanswered, but the evidence suggests that he was only part author. Equally it is doubtful whether the genuine *Essay* was as indecent as has been alleged. Most versions are indecent in the extreme, but the major indecencies are so strained and seemingly isolated that they suggest many not very skilful amendments were made either by those seeking to besmirch Wilkes's name, or by imitators revelling in pornography for its own sake. The obviously Wilkesean parts are not as bawdy as much of Shakespeare and no more indecent than the unexpurgated versions of the *Arabian Nights*.

Commodore Thompson said the *Essay on Woman* was 'not Wilkes's composition'. He does not say whose it was, though others have averred that the text as presented to the Government was a forgery concocted by Kidgell and Curry. Kidgell was certainly capable of the most revolting extravaganza and had been threatened with expulsion from the Church by the Bishop of London on account of his own salacious book, *The Card*. There is, however, no proof that Curry was a conspirator on so low a level.

Whitehead stated that Thomas Potter and Wilkes wrote the *Essay* as a combined effort to parody Pope and deflate his reputation. Their joint effort, completed in 1751, with most of the pornography supplied by Potter, was said to have taken three years to write, in which case the original *Essay* may well have been longer than the generally accepted version which is garnished with notes ascribed satirically to Bishop Warburton, Pope's friend. But there is nothing in this copy of the work which bears either Wilkes's or Potter's name; it is entirely pseudonymous and could hardly be otherwise unless the joke of the notes by Warburton were to lose their point.

The MSS. of a poem of the same title is in the British Museum. It is far shorter than the other *Essay*, and, though printed under Wilkes's name in his lifetime and never disavowed by him, would appear to be either a parody of the original or an utterly spurious copy. Lord Mahon accepted this effort as the original work and it is listed under Wilkes's name at the British Museum, but several literary experts deny that it is the work of either Potter or Wilkes.

This MSS. opens thus:

> 'Awake, my Sandwich, leave all meaner joys
> To Charles and Bob and those true poetic boys.
> Let us, since life can little more supply,
> Then just to kiss, to procreate and die.'

'Charles and Bob' is an obvious reference to Charles Churchill and Robert Lloyd. It is a tedious poem, distinguished neither for elegance nor even Rabelaisian wit.

'The arms of man is woman's proper home,' argues this lascivious but heavy-handed bard, and, continuing in a vein which is reminiscent of an Edwardian paper-back love novelette, he writes of:

> 'The grasp divine, th' emphatic, thrilling squeeze,
> The throbbing, panting breasts and trembling knees;
> The tickling motion, the enlivening flow,
> The rapturous shiver and dissolving – Oh !'

Another imposture, implying that it was a 'genuine copy of *The Essay on Woman*' was published in London at the end of 1763, ascribed on the title page to 'J. W., Senator'. Yet another, published in Paris and sold as a pamphlet, was translated in London ten years later, including the following jingle:

> 'The King was in his counting house, adding up his wealth;
> The Queen was in her boudoir, amusing of herself;
> Poor Wilkes he was in Paris, solaced by Corradini,
> While Despencer down at Mednam languished *in limine*.'[1]

There are grounds for believing that Whitehead revised the Wilkes-Potter version of the *Essay*; his contributions must have been a delightful *potpourri* of the sublime and the salacious, for Whitehead once he set pen to paper couldn't portray a whore without making her seem a virgin.

Everything points to Potter as the main author of the *Essay*. It was he who showed it to the elder Pitt, who, according to the correspondence of the Duke of Grafton, 'admired it for its wit and fancy.' Even staid Horace Walpole, that arch literary impostor so beloved of the neo-Georgian literary circles, commended its 'superb gifts of satire'.

But the truth is that the *Essay* had been discussed in literary circles for more than ten years before the charge was made against Wilkes. Many liked the idea of knocking the idolators of Pope, others, more irreverent, approved the satire on Dr. Warburton, Bishop of Gloucester, who had sponsored Pope's *Essay on Man*. But, when Potter died and Wilkes became a member of the Brotherhood, he revised the manuscript and adapted it to suit the requirements of

1. An eighteenth-century Latin version of the entrance to the womb.

the Franciscans. The latter version of the *Essay* was almost certainly intended for them. Wilkes is said to have recited the new work to the Brothers at Medmenham, where Sandwich was among the loudest in acclaiming it.

When, as a result of Sandwich's attack, it was learned that the *Essay* had been intended solely for the delectation of members of the Order of 'Saint' Francis, the society achieved notoriety far and wide. Kearsley, Wilkes's chief printer, had been asked to print twelve copies of the *Essay* 'for Medmenham', but for some reason he did not finish the job and turned it over to Curry. Curry may or may not have known whom the copies were for, but in agreeing to conspire with Kidgell he may have been influenced by the fact that he had not received payment from Wilkes. It was always assumed that the twelve copies were for the 'Twelve Apostles' or the 'inner circle', but Curry produced thirteen. Whether he printed this extra copy to pass on to Kidgell, or whether it was a special copy intended for Dashwood is uncertain. But it is undisputed that Wilkes had no intention whatsoever of publishing the *Essay* for profit or for distribution to the general public. Thus the pamphlet produced by Kidgell, far from stamping out a scandal, only served to give publicity to something that would otherwise never have become known outside a limited circle.

Some versions of this work contain allusions to the Brotherhood and there are many references, however veiled, to its members. The Greek lettering which appeared on a phallic statue at West Wycombe Park was reproduced in the *Essay*. This was translated by Kidgell in the same way as by Hall Stevenson as 'Saviour of the World', thus making the basis for an accusation of blasphemy. Wilkes's reply to this was that 'this translation fully demonstrates your illiteracy and ignorance and total lack of scholarship. These words have no reference to Christ and therefore the allusion is a blasphemy of your own and not of the author of *Essay on Woman*. The inscription is found on an ancient palace of a date of greater antiquity than Christ.'

It should be noted that Wilkes's attitude to the charges of blasphemy and libel was largely concerned with refuting what had been read into the text. He neither confirmed nor disavowed that he was author. It was an ambiguous attitude that in no way helps posterity to solve the mystery of *The Essay*. But in Paris, where Wilkes was less discreet and more inclined to talk, the impression was gained both by English visitors and French *literateurs* that the version which was entirely Wilkes's own work contained many detailed references to the Medmenhamites and what went on at their gatherings. Such detailed references certainly do not appear either in the original work by Potter and Wilkes, the poem at the British Museum, the MSS. in the Dyce Library at South Kensington, or any other supposed copies.

It is therefore possible that, when the storm against Wilkes broke over *The North Briton* article, some of the Medmenhamites decided that the version most concerned with them ought to be destroyed. Thus the genuine Wilkesean version may have been amended so as to delete obvious references to the Franciscans and, by careful editorship by Kidgell, rewritten to portray Wilkes in the worst possible light.

In Paris Wilkes spent a good deal of time with Jean-François Ducis, an imitator of Shakespeare. Ducis referred to the *Essay* as 'a lusty saga . . . revealing the philosophy of a society of monks founded on the code of the Abbey Thélème, in which the supreme symbol was the *Idolum Tentiginis* of the ancient Romans and Greeks'. This is certainly a reference to the 'Saviour of the World' inscription, as translated by Kidgell. Ducis could hardly have obtained this information from anyone other than Wilkes.

What may have enraged Sandwich more than anything else was the fact that the copy of the work produced by Kidgell was dedicated to that celebrated courtesan, Fanny Murray.[1] Bleackley, in his *Ladies Fair and Frail,* stated that the work was 'written many years before (*presumably before the charge against Wilkes*), when Fanny, the beauty of Bath, was the toast of the hour.' Now Fanny, long after she had been seduced by Jack Spencer at the age of twelve and subsequently adopted by Nash, had been Sandwich's

1. Also Fanny Ross, wife of actor David Ross.

mistress. By that time the former flower seller was a leading light of the demi-monde of London's West End.

Not only was this copy, which is in the Dyce Library at South Kensington, dedicated to Fanny Murray, but it begins with the words 'Awake my Fanny' instead of 'Awake my Sandwich'.

In drawing attention to the *Essay* in the Lords and bringing ridicule on himself, Sandwich provoked a revival of extracts from the original *Essay*, which were circulated in the clubs and around the hostelries of Covent Garden. Why did Sandwich choose to lay himself open to ridicule? Was it ungovernable anger against Wilkes, or was it to detract attention from the genuine *Essay*, which he had had destroyed? If one accepts the statement that the Minute Book of the Brotherhood was destroyed by Sandwich, there is good reason to believe that he wanted to obliterate all written records of the society.

When it was known that the *Essay* was dedicated to Fanny Murray, Philip Carteret Welt, the Treasury Solicitor, went scampering down to Drury Lane to obtain all copies of surreptitiously printed extracts from the work. All Fanny's lovers were in a state of terror lest their indiscretions were about to be made public.

All the rapscallion pornographic pamphleteers proceeded to cash in on the rumour that Fanny Murray was the heroine of the *Essay* and innumerable 'absolutely authenticated quotations from the Amours of Fanny Murray and her Monkish Friends of Mednam' were hawked around. Even the eighteenth century advertising fraternity exploited the situation. Cordials for women (mostly laced plentifully with cheap gin) had for years been sold under such fanciful titles as 'Oil of Venus', 'Strip me Naked', 'Cupid's Eye-Wash' and 'Lay Me Down Softly'. To this Georgian version of the twentieth century's 'gin and sin' were added 'Fanny Murray's Pick-Me-Up', 'Fanny Murray's Nettle Juice' and 'Gin and Fanny Sandwich'.

The climax came when Fanny's 'double' in *The Beggar's Opera* spoke the words: '. . . that Jenny should peach me I owned surprised me'. Gusts of laughter held up the performance for several minutes; from then on Sandwich was nicknamed 'Jemmy Twitcher' to the end of his days. In 1770 a book was published entitled *The Life, Adventures, Intrigues and Amours of the Celebrated Jemmy Twicher*, by J. Brough.

By 1770 John Wilkes had seen the seesaw of fortune go up and down again. In 1776 he returned to London in defiance of his outlawry and had been elected as M.P. for Middlesex. He was again expelled from the House of Commons and imprisoned for two years. But, volatile and undismayed, he fought his way back into public life. On his release from prison he championed the City of London in its contests with Court and Parliament, was elected Lord Mayor and upheld the power of the law during the Gordon Riots.

Thereafter Wilkes was accepted as almost, if not quite, an elder statesman. The old antagonisms faded and in 1774 he was re-elected to represent Middlesex, remaining its member until he retired in 1790. Whatever his faults – and they were many – he was a courageous, far-sighted and able Member of Parliament and a founder of the true Radical tradition. Indeed, in contrast, Charles James Fox seems a feeble, emaciated shadow-boxer of Georgian political life.

CHAPTER 9

THE MYSTERY OF THE 'NUNS' OF MEDMENHAM

ONE of the most remarkable features of the society of 'Saint' Francis is that, while it is relatively easy to identify the male members, the secret of their feminine companions has been well and truly guarded.

There are no documents in existence which reveal the identity of any of the 'Nuns' and neither the Dashwood Papers at the Bodleian Library nor those at Aylesbury Museum throw any light on the matter. Nobody who has previously attempted to investigate the history of the club has produced a list of either known or suspected 'Nuns'.

Johnston referred to 'the slaves of their lusts' as being recruited from brothels. If these women were hired anonymously from London bordellos and sent back to their keepers each time the Medmenham revels ended, this in itself could explain why nothing was known of their identity.

But it is certainly erroneous to suggest that all the 'companions' of the Brothers were recruited from brothels. Mr. Francis Dashwood tells us that 'Medmenham Abbey was used at weekends throughout most of the year, whilst about twice each summer a Chapter or Full Meeting, lasting several days, was convened. On these occasions "nuns" were introduced ... At first these "nuns" consisted of wives of local squires, but when their husbands discovered what was happening and objected, less reputable women were procured from London.'

The author of *Nocturnal Revels* corroborates this. '... every member is allowed to introduce a lady "of a cheerful, lively disposition who embraces a general hilarity". The Ladies in the intervals of their repasts may make select parties among themselves or entertain one another, or alone, with reading,

152

musick, tambour work, etc. . . . . The ceremony of admission is performed in a chapel allotted for that purpose.

'The Ladies consider themselves as the lawful wives of the Bretheren during their stay within monastic walls; every Monk being scrupulous not to infringe upon the nuptial alliance of any other Brother.'

The author inferred that the utmost secrecy concerning these 'alliances' was preserved. 'No Lady may be taken by surprise either by her husband or any other relation. They are admitted in masks and do not unmask till all the Bretheren have passed them in review, that they may avoid, if they judge it expedient, meeting with an unwelcome acquaintance. In this case no *éclaircissement* is required from them, but they may retire without making any apology or revealing themselves to any but their temporary husband.'

Such precautions would certainly not have been taken if the 'nuns' had been recruited solely from brothels. Probably because of the association of the word 'nun' with the inmate of a bagnio, writers assumed wrongly that the women all came from the stews of the West End. Wallace C. Brown, biographer of Charles Churchill, wrote of the Monks importing 'London prostitutes dressed up as "nuns" to take part in their services . . . Churchill, who later had political as well as personal reasons for doing so, never tired of attacking the activities of most of the club members.'

Certainly Churchill gave the impression of being disgusted with the Medmenham orgies, but he nevertheless played a not inconsiderate part in them, though not one of the 'Inner Circle'. And, as the correspondence of Wilkes and Churchill reveals, the latter was as promiscuous an amorist as any of them: 'what I imagined to be St. Anthony's fire turns out to be St. Cytherea's', he once confided to Wilkes.

But Churchill, while he may have been complaisant about visits to stews, or casual liaisons with ladies of easy virtue, also had in him a strong streak of romantic idealism. He could on occasion wax sentimentally about women; in his verse the word 'womanhood' was frequently used as an idealization of maidenhood. There could even be a hint that some of the 'Nuns' were maids in his diatribe on Medmenham that includes these lines:

> 'Whilst Womanhood in habit of a nun
> At Mednam lies, by backwood monks undone;
> A nation's reckoning like an alehouse score,
> Whilst Paul the Aged chalks behind the door.'

There is a slight puzzle about this verse. Some sources, including contemporary editions of Churchill's works, give the word 'backwood' as 'backward'. It may not seem to matter much, but it is intriguing to ponder on what Churchill meant to convey by this phrase. If the word should read 'backward', did he infer his contempt for the mentality of the 'Monks', or has the verse some subtler meaning?

That 'the monastery (*Medmenham*) was not destitute of the aid of the Faculty of medicine and obstetrics' was the claim made in *Nocturnal Revels*. 'In case Ladies want to retreat temporarily from the world' medical aid was provided for them. Apparently there were births arising out of members' club-time activities, for this chronicler of bawdry mentioned that 'Offspring are styled "The Sons and Daughters of Saint Francis" ' and that they became 'officers and domestic in the seminary'. If these statements are to be believed, the club can justly claim to have created its own system of social security for 'Nuns' and offspring. In a period when rakes were not noted for such forethought and kindly consideration, this is one of the good marks which Paul Whitehead might well have chalked up 'behind the door'!

The club's doctor could have been Dr. Bates, who was Dashwood's doctor to the end of his days; he had the advantage of living in the vicinity. It is true that this doctor indignantly refuted the 'scandalous accusations' against the Brotherhood, but this need not be attributed to hypocrisy. For if he were father confessor, medical adviser and midwife to the club, he could also justly claim that the members honoured any untoward results of their frolics and follies.

The only other man who may have been honorary doctor to the club was Dr. Thompson, court physician to Frederick, Prince of Wales, and friend of Bubb Dodington and Paul

Whitehead. Johnston said that Dr. Thompson was Dodington's Mephistopheles, that he wrote a book in praise of vice and then declared it was 'entirely derived from his patron's conversation'. But Dr. Thompson died in 1760 and, as he lived at Twickenham, it is improbable that he was the Medmenham doctor. In any case there is no proof that he was a member of the society.

One suggested source of recruitment for the 'Nuns' was Mother Stanhope's bagnio near Drury Lane. Dashwood is said to have had 'shares' in this establishment, but this is not borne out by the facts. It was not the tradition even for rakes to be procurers for the purposes of financial gain, nor is there any known instance of this. Mother Stanhope was known by the nickname of 'Hell-Fire' Stanhope, and some chroniclers may have put one and one together and called it four. The epithet of 'Hell-Fire' was not originally applied because of any association with Dashwood, but as a direct result of her liaison with Lord Wharton, president of the original Hell-Fire Club.

Mother Stanhope was at the height of her notoriety when Dashwood was a youth. His chief amatory rendezvous in London were the notorious Rose Tavern, much favoured by several Franciscans, and such establishments as Moll King's, Mrs. Goadby's 'nunnery' and Charlotte Hayes's bagnio. Of these the likeliest to have been a recruiting agency for the Brotherhood was the last-named, sometimes grandiloquently referred to as the 'Abbey of Santa Carlotta'.

'Santa Carlotta' was almost a legend among the rakes of eighteenth-century London and her clientele included many of the best-known figures in the land. Each morning, according to the author of *Satan's Harvest Home,* she 'took her rounds to all the inns to see what Youth and Beauty the Country had sent to London . . . when she found a fresh and pretty rural lass she tricked her up with patch and paint – a creature whom she always called a milliner or a parson's daughter'.

'Santa Carlotta always had a stock of virgins in store at King Street,' declared Sandwich. 'She supplies the Stock Exchange with real, immaculate maidenheads.'

George Selwyn was one of her most frequent visitors. The author of *Nocturnal Revels* quoted from an invitation card sent to him by 'Santa Carlotta', which read: 'Mrs. Hayes presents her most respectful compliments and takes the liberty to acquaint . . . that tomorrow evening at 7 p.m. Twelve Beautiful Nymphs, unsullied and untainted, will perform the celebrated rites of Venus as practised at Otaheite under the instruction and tuition of Queen Oberea in which character Mrs. Hayes will appear upon this occasion.'

There is almost a Medmenhamite ring about this piece of description, and it is not without significance that Wilkes on one occasion mentioned 'Cyprian parties *à la* Santa Carlotta and Tahitian fertility rites' at Brotherhood meetings.

The author of *Nocturnal Revels* quoted extensively from what he claimed was Mrs. Hayes's diary. It included such business assignments as 'January 9. A maid for Alderman —. Nell Blossom, about nineteen, has not been in company these four days and was prepared for a state of vestalship last night.

'Colonel —. A modest woman. Mrs. Mitchell's cook-maid being just come from the country and a new face? Or the Countess La Fleur from Seven Dials? Her flash man, La Fleur, must dress her to the best advantage.

'Dr. —. After church is over.'

These were sordid and flamboyant, rumbustuous and carnal days in the West End, with pickpockets and thugs wandering abroad at night and pimps and touts plying their trade all day. The working classes were mostly gin-sodden and large numbers of them were completely un-employable and imbecilic. Vice as an industry was the inevitable result. Clubmen not only exchanged information on the talents of their respective mistresses, but were often only too pleased to swap them with friends. This they did not in any vicious manner, but as one man would offer another hospitality. A letter dated 23 August, 1748, ad-dressed from 'The King's Arms Tavern at four o'clock in the afternoon', signed by one Edmund Easy (possibly an

appropriate psuedonym, this) and dispatched to Jack
Spencer, stated:

'Dear Molly,
    On sight hereof permit the Bearer to immediately enter
a Pair of Holland Sheets with you; and let him have in-
gress, egress and regress to your person; in such manner
as to him shall seem meet, for the space of twenty-four
hours, and no longer, and place it to the account of —
your kind and confident Keeper.'

There was a postscript which added: 'Child, go through
all your exercises and evolutions as well for your own as my
credit.'

Spencer has not been listed as other than a 'possible
member' of the Brotherhood, but there are some grounds
for believing that he was 'Brother John of Westminster'.

Such research into the stews and salons of London, while
revealing in its portrait of the private life of some sections
of the fashionable world, does not carry one nearer to
identifying any of the 'Nuns'. The most one can assume is
that Mrs. Hayes was a procurer for Medmenham; one
entry in her diary read: 'June 19, 1759. Twelve Vestals for
the Abbey. Something discreet and Cyprian for the Friars.'[1]

But Mrs. Hayes was discreet and doubtless she ensured
that the anonymity of the 'Vestals' was preserved.

Fanny Murray once boasted that she had 'waited on the
Monks at Mednam', but there is no confirmation of this.
After leaving Bath she came to London where Mrs. Stanhope decked her out as a parson's daughter to such good
effect that she soon became Sandwich's mistress. But,
though Jack Spencer, her earliest seducer, was a friend of
Dashwood in his youth, her name has not been linked with
the founder of the Brotherhood. When the notorious
'Arise, my Fanny' version of the *Essay on Woman* was made
public, it was generally assumed that Fanny had been one

1. *Memoirs of a London Abbess.*

of the 'Nuns', but as Wilkes remained silent on this point, it cannot be accepted as evidence.

Sir Max Pemberton's research into the history of the society has already been mentioned, and, apart from introducing the theme into his novel, *Sir Richard Escombe,* he claimed that a rule of conduct had been laid down in the club's constitution – 'For the safeguarding of our honour it shall be decreed that any Brother who draws sword upon another in the name of a woman, shall, by his own hand, pay forfeit of his life before twenty-four hours have passed.'

Sir Max assured the author that he had seen documentary evidence of this rule of conduct, but he could not recall the source. He believed the information was obtained from 'private papers belonging to someone at Bisham Abbey'. These could have been the Vansittart Papers. There is, however, no indication that such a rule was ever invoked by members of the society.

In Dashwood's life many women figured, but, except for his wife, they are shadowy, elusive creatures who have left behind no legends of their association with him. Women talked far less then than they do now about their amatory adventures. As for Dashwood, while Sandwich, Selwyn and their associates were nearer to the 'Roaring Boy' tradition, loudly proclaiming their venal conquests, he was much more reticent. There was something incredibly furtive about his *affaires* with women from the still unexplained escapade with the Tsarina of Russia to his last days with Mrs. Barry. Of the other rakes of this age of frankness among men there are innumerable anecdotes, well substantiated by correspondence and diary jottings in Boswellian fashion. But of Dashwood there is nothing at all except for brief innuendoes by Walpole about Miss Bateman and Lady Mary Wortley-Montagu, and such bald statements as, 'He was the lover of Lucy Cooper, who was lewder than all the whores of Charles II's reign, and the keeper of Elizabeth Roach.' It is probable that he struck up a friendship with Lord Bute through the acquaintance with Mary Wortley-Montagu.

There are also hints that he had an *affaire* with Frances

Anne, Viscountess Vane, whose *Memoirs of a Lady of Quality* were first published in Tobias Smollett's novel, *Peregrine Pickle*.

Sir Francis was also involved in a very curious episode in France, when he tried to establish that he had two legitimate children. His attempt failed, as a private detective followed him and produced a dated account to show that both children were illegitimate.

But by far the most baffling and intriguing account of Dashwood's love life and one which certainly poses a problem of identity of one of the 'Nuns' is contained in the works of Hall Stevenson.

This is *The Confessions of Sir F— of Medmenham and of The Lady Mary, his Wife*.[1] This must have been written prior to 1762, judging from the reference to Francis by his earlier title and from the correspondence between Hall Stevenson and John Wilkes. In a letter written in 1762 by Stevenson to Wilkes the former wrote: 'Do give me a line with your Absolution for my transgressions to Saint Francis, and a hint at the world to come.'

Wilkes had asked Stevenson for the MSS. of 'a collection of . . .[2] all kind hymning the praises of your friend'. The word *praises* was doubtless used sarcastically, a favourite trick with Wilkes; it was almost certainly an indirect reference to Stevenson's *Confessions of Sir F— of Medmenham*. This shows that Wilkes and Stevenson, as fellow Whigs, corresponded about the club, and it would seem that Wilkes was gathering more information than the inscription on statues at Medmenham and West Wycombe provided. These two men and Walpole were all in league with one another and Stevenson persisted in a lengthy vendetta with Dashwood, despite the help and advice he had received from that quarter. The worst of his diatribes against Francis appeared in the collected works of Stevenson, published posthumously.

Referring to Dashwood the *Confessions*, which are entirely in verse, include the following:

1. The Works of John Hall Stevenson (3 vols., 1795).
2. The actual word used here is indecipherable in the original.

'Like a Hotspur young cock, he began with his mother,
Cheer'd three of his sisters one after another;
And oft tried little Jen, but gain'd so little ground,
Little Jen lost her patience and made him compound.'

The confessions of Lady Mary are more candid. They describe an extraordinary amatory triangle involving Lady Mary, 'a masculine nun' and a 'frier' (presumably 'friar'). It is the last verse only of these 'confessions' which has some significance:

'Between frier and knight, my Lesbian's brother,
I was like to become an unfortunate mother;
But by her assistance and skill I miscarried,
And at last, through her means, to Sir Francis was married.'

It is all rather on the level of 'There was a young girl from Khartoum'. If the above verse suggests anything at all it is that the doctor of the Franciscans may not have been either Dr. Bates or Dr. Thompson, but a midwife or amateur female abortionist. But, however wearisome the 'ifs' and 'buts', it is necessary to probe this doggerel, if only to analyse its cowardly innuendoes. Who was 'Lady Mary'? If Hall Stevenson was basing his verses on fact – and, as has already been seen, there is proof that he had first-hand knowledge of what went on at Medmenham – then it seems obvious that 'Lady Mary' was one of the 'Nuns'. The reference to 'friers' and 'nuns', the dedication of the poem to 'Sir F— of Medmenham' with the emphasis on the site of the Abbey rather than on Dashwood's domicile, together with the documentary evidence of Hall Stevenson's correspondence with Wilkes and Sterne, all suggest that this poem was intended to portray some of the scandals of the Franciscans.

One presumes that the author used the phrase 'Lady Mary, his Wife' in the sense that the Nocturnal Reveller talked about 'the lawful wives of the Bretheren during their stay within monastic walls'. He could not have been referring to Lady Dashwood, whose name was Sarah and whose private life appears to have been beyond reproach.

It is possible that 'Lady Mary' was a fictitious character introduced for the sake of telling a story, but the vogue of the era in such poetic narratives was to tell a factual story; indeed, the more Rabelaisian the subject the more likely it was to be true – or, at least, intended to be true. It must be remembered that such poems were composed to enliven after-dinner drinking bouts, when the port was flowing freely. They could not have been printed for fear of libel. The chief function of the Demoniacs Club was for its members to assemble at Crazy Castle in Yorkshire and to sit and listen to the *Crazy Tales* specially composed for them by Hall Stevenson. Doubtless the *Confessions* was one of the Rabelaisian tales with which he used at the same time to amuse his guests and satisfy his own ego.

This poem is verbally infelicitious, banal and, though describing some unusual sexual permutations, has neither the rhythmic and onomatopaeic merit of Restoration wit, nor the picturesquely rounded humour of Rabelais. As a story it is obscure, badly told and utterly pointless unless those for whom it was intended could read into it more than what it says. If this merely related to some squalid transaction between Sir Francis and one of the 'Nuns', it is difficult to see why it should have been given such an intriguing title.

Therefore, it seems reasonable to assume that Hall Stevenson was either indulging in malicious lying, or that he was hinting at some dark and abnormal secret in Sir Francis's love life – some incident which the founder of the Brotherhood wanted to be hushed up, but one which would cause a sensation when revealed to his enemies. This must have referred to something which dated back long before 1762. Was this the secret which John Wilkes tried to persuade Hall Stevenson to divulge? If it were, then it has remained a secret for more than 200 years and all one can do today is to examine the various tangled clues for a possible solution.

In the first of the verses quoted it is clear beyond doubt that Hall Stevenson was implying that Sir Francis had had incestuous intercourse with his mother and three of his sisters. And the rest of the poem seems to allege that his mother was one of the 'Nuns' of Medmenham. This is a scurrilous accusation which, inasmuch as it concerns his mother, can easily be refuted. The Lady Mary Fane who became the second Lady Dashwood[1] and father of Francis II, died on 19 August, 1710, in her thirty-fifth year, when her son was only two years old.

One would be inclined to dismiss this puerile piece of pornography as malicious insanity, but for the fact that Hall Stevenson, though an eccentric character and the original Eugenius of *Tristam Shandy*, was also a shrewd, well educated and practical man. One must, therefore, reject the idea that he was so stupid as to invent this story of incestuous relationship, knowing that it could so easily be repudiated. Also the correspondence of Wilkes, Sterne and Stevenson shows that there was some mystery at Medmenham which all three wished to unravel: to quote Sterne, 'there are some flagitious designs for a peculiarly oriental mode of living at Medmenham, by no means the least of which concerns the identity of some of the Stars who are Mother, Sisters and Wives of the founder.'

Dashwood's father, the first Sir Francis, had four wives, the first three of whom were all named Mary. Thus Stevenson might have confused one of the stepmothers with Dashwood's mother. The third wife was Mary, daughter of Major King, who died in December 1719 also in her thirty-fifth year. It is hard to imagine that 'Lady Mary' could have referred to this stepmother, as this would mean she seduced her stepson before he was eleven years old.

The fourth wife was Elizabeth, daughter of Thomas Windsor, Earl of Plymouth, by whom he had no issue. Very little is known about her and, oddly, she was not commemorated at West Wycombe Church,[1] as were the second and third wives. It is also curious that the second and third wives are honoured by monuments in the Mausoleum, depicting both with eyes turned to heaven and surrounded by

1. The first Lady Dashwood (Mary, daughter of John Jennings of Westminster) died in 1694.
1. She died in 1737.

weeping cupids, an unusual choice of memorial even in the sometimes bizarre eighteenth-century fashion of memorials. Even more curious is the fact that the inscriptions are brief and purely factual, making no reference to the virtues of the two ladies, an almost unparalleled omission in this period.

There can be no grounds for suggesting that Stevenson's poem referred to the first Sir Francis and not his son. The title of the work – 'Sir F— of Medmenham' – makes this abundantly clear, for Francis I had no associations either with the abbey or the village of this name.

Was 'Lady Mary' a mistaken reference to Elizabeth, the fourth wife? Young Francis would have been in his early 'teens at the time of this marriage, and there is evidence that she had a remarkable hold on his affections. Curiously, too, she was nearly always referred to in West Wycombe as 'Lady Mary', probably from force of habit. Thomas Langley, who made a complete list of the inhabitants of Medmenham for the year 1748–49,[1] mentioned the 'fine London wife of Richard Edgerley', who lived at Newlock. She was the only woman living in the district to whom he drew special attention; in most cases he merely gave the man's name and added 'and wife', 'and mother', or 'and daughter', making no comment at all. About fifty years ago demolition work in the village brought to light a quantity of diaries, letters and bills of the period 1748–54.

These includes some significant items of information. One recorded that 'Sophia Edgerley did this day report to the Lady Mary for a situation at the Abbey'. It was a barely legible, unsigned diary entry and the date might have been either 1751 or 1754. Judging by the various bills found among the papers the writer of the diary was a tailor – possibly 'Mr. Townsend, a London tailor at Medmenham', as he was listed by Langley.

Another item indicated that 'eight ladies' white habits, made to original design' were delivered to the Abbey. Were these the 'Nuns' ' robes?

One must reject entirely the outrageous allegations of incestuous conduct made by Hall Stevenson. Because there

1. MSS. in the Library of the Society of Antiquaries.

have been so many equally wild tirades against Sir Francis and the Medmenhamites; this malicious indictment in doggerel has been thoroughly examined by the author. Wilkes was obviously disgusted by Stevenson's failure to reveal any further 'evidence' and by his refusal to send him the collection of his poetic diatribes against Dashwood. One's impression is that Stevenson was insanely jealous of Dashwood, that he was angered because he was not admitted to the 'inner circle' of the Brotherhood and baffled by the effective methods employed to keep secret the identity of the 'Nuns'.

The fact that the 'Nuns' wore masks and that rules were carefully formulated to hide their identity rather suggests that some of them had good reason to remain anonymous – probably because some may have been wives or sisters of male members. It is not improbable that some of Dashwood's half-sisters attended meetings of the Brotherhood, wearing nuns' habits, and Stevenson may have concocted his wicked libels on some tittle-tattle to this effect. Dashwood had four sisters living (one, Henrietta, died when very young) during the heyday of the society – two named Mary, Susanna and Rachel.

'Lady Mary' might have been Mary Walcott, half-sister to Sir Francis. There is a painting of her at West Wycombe House wearing Divan Club attire and marked 'Sultana Walcotona'. If she were a member of the rakish Divan Club, she may well have been one of the 'Nuns' of Medmenham. This seems to be the likeliest solution of this intriguing problem and much more probable than the other possible theory – that Hall Stevenson's mystery woman was Lady Mary Wortley-Montagu. The last-named is also depicted in a costume of the Divan Club in a painting at West Wycombe, but she would have been approaching sixty when the Brotherhood was founded and past seventy when she returned to England from Venice in 1762.

Mlle Perrault has this to say on the subject of the 'Nuns' of Medmenham:

'While on a tour of England it was with the greatest interest that I paid a visit to West Wycombe Caves, of which I had heard so much through my family associations.

'English local guide and history books mention by name many of the "Monks" of the notorious Order of "Saint" Francis, but none, so far as I have been able to discover, refers to any of the "Nuns". It may, therefore, be of some interest if I tell you that I have always understood that an ancestor of mine was one of them.

'She was of English birth and known to members of the Order as "Saint" or "Sister" Agnes. I presume that Agnes was the name chosen for her by the society, as her real name seems to have been Mary. I do not know her surname, but she was apprenticed to a bookseller named Coustance, who had, I believe, taken over the publishing business of Edmund Curll in Covent Garden.

'She eventually married an ancestor of mine named Léon Perrault and spent the remaining years of her life in France, where she died in 1850. Her story, as it has been passed down in my family, is that she was a girl of singularly ethereal beauty; she had what the French called the beauty of *tristesse*, and even when she was quite old her face was still elfine and glowed with a vivid spiritual quality ...

'She appealed strongly to Paul Whitehead, the poet and a member of the Order of "St." Francis, and he chose her as the "First Lady of the Order", where she was installed as Sister Agnes.

'Possibly I may seem prejudiced in defending the honour of an ancestor, but I have always understood that her role in that strange society was a strictly Platonic one. Whitehead originally desired her for a mistress, but Sir Francis Dashwood had other ideas. He was so impressed by her modesty and virtue, so awed by her beauty, that he had the idea of educating her rather in the same fashion as Eliza Doolittle in Shaw's play *Pygmalion*.

'So startled was he by her likeness to a Madonna that he had her hidden away from his fellow libertines. It is said that he made her the "Saint" of the Order, but with the

165

understanding that she alone would preserve a vow of celibacy.

'She must have been bound by some oath of secrecy, for apparently she would not reveal any of the society's rites.

'She spoke of Dashwood, Whitehead, Sandwich, Wilkes and Churchill. For Dashwood she had a great veneration and regarded him almost as a father; she considered him to be a much superior person to the other "Monks". Whitehead she regarded as a foolish, but not unkind old roué, who kept his pledge not to molest her. Wilkes she saw occasionally during his exile in Paris after she herself had married.

'From all she said Charles Churchill must have been one of her most fervent admirers. He set her up as his model of womanhood and much of his hatred of the "Monks" was born of a fear that they would seduce her. He refused to believe that she was not being held prisoner against her will by some mysterious "Abbess" whom Dashwood had installed in the caves. Agnes kept a copy of a verse which Churchill had written about her.

'Much of the talk about necromancy and satanism was nonsense, according to Agnes, and due to the practical jokes which Dashwood and Wilkes revelled in. Dashwood invented the tale of a mysterious "Abbess" who lived in a secret cell in the caves and presided over the "Nuns". On one occasion he led the "Monks" to a hole in the wall of one of the passages and let them peep at a repulsive witch's face dimly lit by the slender flames of a taper. But the witch's face was not human, but simply a mask which Dashwood had placed there.

'I am afraid this history is fragmentary and inconclusive. "Sister" Agnes never revealed any of the names of the "Nuns", a subject which she deliberately avoided. I believe she may have acted as a nurse to some of them during their pregnancies and perhaps for this reason she regarded their secrets as sacred. Round about 1766–68 she must have been released from her vow of celibacy by Dashwood (then Lord le Despencer) and she left the country to live in France. I cannot say why she was released from her vow, but as her husband was a friend of the Chevalier D'Eon, who knew

Sir Francis intimately, this may have had something to do with it.

'The identity of "Lady Mary" in Hall Stevenson's poem is, as you say, a difficult problem. Agnes's real name was certainly Mary; it is therefore possible that she was at some time known as "Lady Mary". Certainly from all I have heard of her she had no illicit liaison with Dashwood or any of the other "Monks". The account of her life, such as it is, was handed down in my family from her son and she was regarded as a meticulously truthful old lady and most saintly in her ways.

'My own feeling is that Dashwood maintained the myth of a mysterious Abbess who "ruled" over the "Nuns" and dwelt in a secret cell in the cave, and that this led some people to speculate on her identity. Perhaps Hall Stevenson thought Dashwood had something to hide and so invented the tale that the Abbess with the witch's face was Dashwood's mother.

'I believe that in the caves Dashwood had arranged one secret cell with a tableau of "Nuns" carved out of wax and, when members had had too much to drink, he let them peep through a hole at this tableau and made them believe they were real. All these practical jokes may have led to the most remarkable stories. Perhaps in his dotage he liked visitors to think he was still surrounded with beautiful women.'

The further one probes the identity of the 'Nuns' of Medmenham the greater the mystery becomes. To pursue the matter further would be pointless. What is most baffling is that in an age when men were not reticent with one another about their laisons with women and when the most trivial *affaire* was noted down in the greatest detail in diaries and letters, none of the members of the Brotherhood revealed anything of his associations with the ladies of Medmenham. Not even those who described so much else about the society. Even more remarkable is the silence maintaied by at least two of the women directly concerned with club activies – Agnes (or Mary) Perrault and the sole female who survived the orgies and was questioned by Thomas Langley.

Langley, who was buried in Great Marlow churchyard in

1801, could have had no personal knowledge of the society. His *History of the Hundred of Desborough* was published in 1797 and dedicated to Earl Temple. In his chapter on Medmenham he deals very briefly with the Franciscans, suggesting they were not as bad as had been alleged, but admitting that they hardly lived up to the precepts of the original Saint Francis. 'The woman who was their only female domestic is still living and after many inquiries all their transactions may as well be buried in oblivion,' he wrote.

Was this woman the 'fine London wife' of Richard Edgerley, that Sophia Edgerley who accepted 'a situation at the Abbey'?

In his personal copy of *The Hundred of Desborough*, Langley added some thousands of words of handwritten notes and sketches to supplement the printed word. These were obviously intended for posterity and one would have thought that had he learned more of the mysteries of the Franciscans he would have included some notes on this subject.

CHAPTER 10

THE HELL-FIRE CAVES

FOR a county situated so close to the metropolis there are surprising coteries of superstition in Buckinghamshire even today. It is not superstition such as one finds in Cornwall or remote country districts, but tiny, self-sufficient, stubborn bastions of prejudice held in a dogmatic, take-it-or-leave-it manner.

Some observers attribute this Buckinghamshire foible to the influence of Gypsy tribes of two centuries ago. Whatever the cause, it exists and, though not easily discernible to a casual visitor, can quickly be sensed by a sensitive observer of the human scene once he tries to probe local folklore. Nowhere is it more evident than in West Wycombe itself. And one of the ways in which it is manifested is in the slightly hostile attitude of some of the older villagers to what they are pleased to call the Hell-Fire Caves.

It is very difficult to get the villagers to talk about the caves. The older inhabitants seem almost ashamed of them; they become stubbornly silent when questioned about their history. 'Much better an' they weren't opened up again,' one old man said. 'They were better left alone and allowed to be forgotten.'

The older villagers seem to dislike the idea of publicity for something which they vaguely regard as discreditable to the village. When it was suggested that some of the receipts from the caves should go to the funds of St. Lawrence's Church, the vicar banned the idea and revealed a profound abhorrence for the legend of the Monks being linked in any way with the church.

Some villagers display an almost physical antipathy to the caves under West Wycombe Hill. It is almost 'not done' to talk about them. 'I wouldn't go there, if I were you,' said one old soul of seventy. 'Not that I have ever been, or know anything about them, of course. But they're not quite nice.'

Even the pamphlets about St. Lawrence's Church merely refer to 'an artificial cave was dug by Sir Francis Dashwood about 1750. It is said that the Hell-Fire Club used to meet in a room at the end of the cave.' Thus the author of this church pamphlet perpetuates the error that this was a Hell-Fire Club.

The Rev. Arthur Plaisted revealed that the road constructed by Dashwood was made of 'the chalk of prehistoric caves two-hundred yards to the east of the church'. Another authority declared that Dashwood decided to adapt the existing caves, which dated back thousands of years, into a headquarters for the society. There seems little doubt that Dashwood's caves were not the first to be created on this site, and Wooler (an authority on Bucks) told of a pagan altar built on West Wycombe Hill 'in the earliest known times', beneath which was supposed to exist a pagan catacomb.

Thomas Langley, in his *History of the Hundred of Desborough*, said The Hundred took its name from 'a depopulated place of that name in the parish of West Wycombe'. Desborough was a corruption of Denesborough or Danesborough – 'a fortress on a hill designed to stop the ravages of barbarous people'.[1] This Hundred is one of the three Chiltern Hundreds, the others being those of Stoke and Burnham.

An ancient legend of Buckinghamshire tells that in the Middle Ages, when men first attempted to build a church at the foot of the hill, unseen hands destroyed it at night as fast as it was built in day-time. Eventually a 'deep and unearthly voice' told the priest to have the church built on the crest of the hill where it would not be disturbed. This is advanced as the solution to Wilkes's cynical inquiry about why a church should be erected on the crest of the hill 'for the benefit of those at the bottom'.

Such legends, coupled with the hint of a link with prehistoric paganism, must have appealed to Dashwood, though it would seem that his ideas for developing the caves came to

1. The outline of Desborough Castle is still clearly visible from West Wycombe.

him gradually over a period of years. The probability is that originally he only planned the caves as a logical and tidy conclusion to the excavations made for materials for his road, offsetting the utilitarianism of the former by a decorative grotto or folly, according to the fashion of the day. The caves were almost completed by 1753, ten years before the beginning of the break-up of the Medmenhamites, and it is unlikely that the society would have continued throughout this period at Medmenham, had the caves been primarily intended as a new headquarters for the society. In any event, as we shall later see, some functions were continued at Medmenham long after 1763.

The entrance to the caves was built on a platform levelled into the steel chalk hillside and backed by a cliff overgrown with yew trees. Half way up the hill this entrance, built up of flint triangles and pyramids, leading through a large Gothic courtyard, gave the impression of a roofless, ruined church. No doubt this was intentional, not to create the symbol of a church or to recapture the atmosphere of Medmenham (in 1753 there was no need for this), but simply because of the prevailing romanticism which liked its follies to resemble ruined churches.

A low, vaulted passage led northwards deep into West Wycombe Hill. Inside the tunnel the original pick marks can still be seen, for the caves were carved out entirely by hand. The passages extend for a quarter of a mile under the hill – 'cut out in a symbolic and suggestive manner', says one source. The 'suggestive manner' is a reference to the theory that the caves, like the gardens of West Wycombe House, were supposed to be created in the shape of a woman. A map of the underground tunnels does not obviously confirm this, though various ingenious interpretations of the meanings of their twists and turns have been made. Dr. G. B. Gardener, of the Witches' Mill, Castletown, Isle of Man, a student of the occult, claims that the triangular passage deep inside the caves is a 'pubic triangle . . . followed by the womb where it swells out into the Styx'.

There have also been attempts to show that the caves follow an occult pattern, that the triangular passage is a necromantic sign, but there is no evidence to substantiate this other than some devils' heads most skilfully and professionally carved in the chalk. The only other intriguing sign is the enigmatic 'XXIIF' cut high upon the left hand wall about a third of the way along the passages between the robing room and the catacombs. The 'F' may be an abbreviation for Francis, but there is no clue as to what the Roman numerals for twenty-two might mean. The general belief is that it indicated the whereabouts of a legendary secret passage which led off the catacombs. An old village rhyme goes:

'Take twenty steps and rest awhile;
Then take a pick and find the stile
Where once I did my love beguile.'

But before pondering further on the enigma of the Roman numerals, or the intriguing rhyme, let us follow the narrow passage leading from the entrance and so obtain a consecutive idea of the layout of the caves. The dark, cool tunnel is silent and eerie, the eeriness being accentuated by the occasional drip, drip, drip of tiny particles of water from the roof. After turning sharply to the left one comes to a small chamber on the right of the passage called the 'Robing Room'.[1] Here the Brothers were said to have changed into 'the brown habits of the Franciscan Order'. This is of special interest in that at Medmenham they were described as wearing flowing white robes and, on formal occasions, crimson and blue with the silver badge bearing the 'love and friendship' motto. No authority mentions brown robes having been worn at Medmenham, and one wonders whether this change of uniform marked the division of the Franciscans into rival sects after the disputes of 1763. It is a small 'Robing Room' and would only accommodate a few members at a time.

Farther on are the devils' heads carved on the wall, then a huge circular pillar in the middle of the passage, and it is mid-way between this pillar and the catacombs that the sign

1. There is no positive documentary evidence that the 'Robing Room', etc., were the original names.

'XXIIF' is to be seen. The honeycomb of catacombs is really a series of minute, interweaving passages rather like the vaults of a church. Possibly Francis was copying the catacombs of Rome, where the early Christians buried their dead, but this can only be supposition; it is a theory which fits in with his known love of the macabre and passion for ancient Rome. But it is equally possible that these were adapted from the original pagan catacombs mentioned by Wooler. Just past the catacombs, on the left, is the beginning of another passage with steps leading sharply upwards, but it ends after a few yards as abruptly as it began.

There is much conjecture as to whether this was part of a passage connecting the caves with the church, and which, for some reason or other, was ultimately blocked up. An examination of the geographical lay-out above suggests that, if this passage continued upwards in the same direction, it would lead to the Mausoleum, which is close to the Church of St. Lawrence. Whether this was the beginning of the secret passage of legend it is impossible to say, but, if it were blocked up, this was certainly not carried out during the past hundred years.[1] The only alteration made to the caves since they were originally cut, as far as is known, is a small tunnel which by-passes the banqueting hall. Owing to the possibility of pieces of chalk dropping from the ceiling of the banqueting hall, it was decided not to allow visitors to enter it, and a new passage was dug in 1954 by some Yorkshire miners living in High Wycombe. This passage runs round the west side of the banqueting hall and joins up with the old passage on the far side.

After the catacombs the main passage turns at right angles and leads to the banqueting hall, reputed to be the largest man-made chalk cave in the world. Deep in the heart of the hill, it is approximately forty feet in diameter and fifty feet in height. The passage flanking the left-hand side of the banqueting hall should be disregarded in assessing the original plan of this subterranean tavern of revelry. It is

1. The miners who carried out reconstruction work in 1954 were convinced there was a secret passage farther on, indicated by a current of air.

more important to note the four 'Monks' cells' leading off the hall at each quarter of the circle. These cells are described as being for the 'private devotions' of the Monks. Whatever these devotions might have been, the cells hardly allow room for much merriment, and, when curtained off from the banqueting hall must have formed extremely claustrophobic quarters for a 'Monk' and his 'Nun'. Perhaps they were made small for warmth, or perhaps 'Saint' Francis had them planned like confessional boxes as another of his little jokes. As a plan of the caves shows, each cell had a tiny teat-shaped recess at its innermost point. This could have been used as a wardrobe, or for placing a lantern; on the other hand it might have contained some of the suggestive statuary which Sir Francis liked to scatter around in odd corners. This deduction is supported to some extent by the evidence of a bill of 1748, showing items for setting up statuary in the caves and for fixing a stone at their entrance.

On the ceiling of the banqueting hall can still be seen the hook from which once hung a lamp. Judging by the size of the hook it must have been a large lamp, possibly the Rosicrucian lamp originally used at the meetings at the George and Vulture. Dr. Gardener, of Castletown, claims to have the original lamp in his possession. One must rely upon imagination to reconstruct the scenes which were enacted in the banqueting hall in those far-off days, for while there are many contemporary reports of what went on at Medmenham, no detailed records exist of ceremonies in the caves. Neither Wilkes, Walpole nor Johnston refer to the caves, and it is strange that Langley, who devoted so much attention to West Wycombe's history to his book on *The Hundred of Desborough*, made no mention of them. One's impression is that at no time did many of the Brothers assemble together in this subterranean meeting place. Presumably food was prepared at West Wycombe House and brought to the caves, where according to local legend, 'The Devil' was toasted in port after sumptuous repasts.

But it would be unwise to give too free a rein to the imagination. Easy as it is to conjure up a picture of oriental opulence and splendour in the caves, neither their construction, nor their position suggests that luxury prevailed there. The cells must have been exceedingly cramped, the long walk through the winding passages especially irksome for middle-aged roués like Bubb Dodington[1] and Whitehead, while the elimination of cold and damp would present a difficult problem in winter or summer. Apart from all this there is the report that in the society's time an underground stream flowed through parts of the caves. Some have asserted that this stream actually flowed through the banqueting hall, though this seems unlikely.

After the banqueting hall there is a steep slope down hill to a junction where the passage branches off at right angles to right and left, still descending deeper into the hill. Then each branch turns back to join the other and so they form the triangle already mentioned.

From the triangle a single passage leads to the buttery, after which a bridge unexpectedly crosses a strip of ink-black water. This is all that visibly remains of the underground stream which is said to have been wider and deeper 200 years ago – so wide that it 'could only be crossed by boat'. The narrow stream is referred to as the 'Styx',[2] but who played the role of Charon in Francis's time one does not know.

But the 'Styx' and the grimly silent 'cursing well' beside it make an appropriate barrier to the 'Inner Temple' or 'Chapel', the round, vaulted chamber which marks the end of the caves in the very deepest part of the hill. 'What took place here no one really knows,' states the current guidebook to the caves. 'We can only guess at the rites which took place in the secrecy of this subterranean temple.'

Once again there is a hint of black magic. But Mr. Francis Dashwood affirms that the 'Cursing Well' is an innovation dating from 1954 and that the phrase 'unholy water' is fictitious.

Probably the caves were dismantled of all traces of habitation or ceremonial before Lord le Despencer died. If not, then the villagers themselves must have carried away the

1. Bubb Dodington may have died before the caves were used.
2. Chambers' *Book of Days* and Mrs. Lybbe-Powys.

remaining paraphernalia of the Brotherhood as souvenirs. If they did, nothing has been seen of it since. While Medmenham was frequently visited, the caves were neglected or ignored for many years. There were the usual stories that they were haunted and the villagers discouraged anyone from entering them.

Nor did le Despencer's descendants take any interest in the caves for many years. Until he died about twenty years ago, an old man who lived in a cottage nearby looked upon the caves as his own domain, and he took it upon himself to keep the key to them and occasionally, when in the mood, to show visitors around for a modest fee. Most of the stories of the Brotherhood's activities in those winding passages in the bowels of the earth are legends woven by generations of villagers, highly coloured and of dubious authenticity. It is said that the 'Monks' drew their 'unholy water from the 'cursing well', that there was a large slab in the 'Inner Temple' on which the Black Mass was celebrated. In this inner 'unholy of unholies', we are assured, 'the worst wickedness was carried out.'

A variety of reasons caused a gradual rather than a sudden migration from Medmenham Abbey to the caves. The theory that after the episode of the baboon garbed as the Devil a decision was made to quit Medmenham for the caves can be entirely rejected. Wilkes's testimony does not support this, nor does that of Walpole. The fact that there is not much evidence of what went on at Medmenham and so little about the caves may mean that the Brothers who attended functions in the latter were members of the 'Inner Circle' only. They would be the least likely to discuss what went on under West Wycombe Hill.

It should be noted that the caves were six miles distant from Medmenham and much nearer to West Wycombe House than the Abbey. Probably those Brothers who lived nearer West Wycombe than Medmenham occasionally met 'Saint' Francis in the caves, this being a convenient rendezvous. By the late 'fifties the Brotherhood was tending to have a superfluity of members, and perhaps Francis feared that there was a risk of some of the society's secrets being bandied around. For this reason he may have arranged occasional 'Chapters' to be held in the caves.

From 1763 onwards the caves must have seemed a safer and preferable headquarters in view of the notoriety which Medmenham had drawn upon itself following the revelations of Wilkes and the widespread publicity about the society. Possibly, too, with a number of the members not on speaking terms with one another, one faction met in the caves to avoid contact with the dissenters.

What literary references there are to the caves are obscure, yet full of fascinating puzzles. Hall Stevenson, who wrote odes to Dashwood and Sir Thomas Stapleton, made a cryptic hand-written note to one of his poems; it stated 'a query on the strange events which took place under West Wycombe Hill.'

> 'Where can I find a cave to muse
> Upon his lordship's envied glory,
> Which of the Nine dare to refuse
> To tell the strange and recent story?
> Mounting I saw the egregious lord
> O'er all impediments and bars;
> I saw him at Jove's council board
> And saw him stuck among the stars.'

Whether 'the Nine' refers to some of the Franciscans and what the 'strange and recent story' was are, perhaps, matters of idle and inconsequential conjecture. What is of most interest is the reference to 'the stars'. In reading eighteenth-century verse one cannot afford lightly to pass over the frequent references to 'stars'. It is easy to dismiss such a word as a poetic cliché of the period, an overworked word employed by lazy poets. But among rakes the word 'star' was sometimes used to distinguish the more scintillating of the fair sex from their usual company of courtesans, wenches, bawds and harlots. Hall Stevenson, Churchill and Lloyd all used the word in this sense.

In Churchill's poem *The Duellist* he wrote:

'Under the Temple lay a cave;
Made by some guilty, coward slave,
Whose actions fear'd rebuke, a maze
Of intricate and winding ways,
Not to be found without a clue;
One passage only, known to few,
In paths direct led to a cell.
Where Fraud in secret lov'd to dwell,
With all her tools and slaves about her,
Nor fear'd lest honesty should rout her.

In a dark corner, shunning sight
Of Man, and shrinking from the light,
One dull, dim taper thro' the cell
Glimm'ring to make horrible
The face of darkness, she prepares,
Working unseen, all kinds of snares,
With curious, but destructive art;

Here, thro' the eye to catch the heart,
Gay Stars their tinsel beams afford,
Neat artifice to trap a Lord;
There, fit for all whom Folly bred,
With Plumes of Feathers for the head.'

Is there in this obscure verse a further hint of the secret
passage 'not to be found without a clue'? And were the
'Gay Stars' the Nuns of West Wycombe?

Charles Churchill was not normally an obscure poet: his
sense of satire, his zest for attack lent clarity and directness
to his pen. But on those occasions when his idealism was
uppermost and he tried to soar into the heavens on his muse,
he was apt to be dragged down to earth by his own inescap-
able and almost pathological urge to satirize. Every time
he saw a vision of beauty Churchill was haunted by some
malevolent satyr that bewitched his own processes of
thought. Try as he might, he could not help slipping some
sly and often irrelevant satire into his main theme. Thus
an abstract essay into flights of romanticism would also

serve to hide between the lines some subtle satire on a person or institution.

Perhaps some slight clue to this verse may be found in the personality of 'Saint Agnes'. Mlle Perrault writes: 'When I visited West Wycombe I was very interested in the legend of the secret passage, for "Sister Agnes" often spoke of a secret cell, where she had her own quarters in the cave and which had access to the church on the hill. It would seem that at some time this passage was blocked up.

'There is a suggestion that "Sister Agnes" used to meet a clergyman in this passage and that he came to visit her from the church. He is supposed to have been hoplessly in love with her; she refused to break her vow and marry him, and in consequence of this he drowned himself.'

Has this story any connexion with the drowning of Edmund Duffield in the Thames off Medmenham, or the story about Timonthy Shaw? Local legend, the strange rhyme and the testimony of Mlle Perrault would all seem to confirm the existence of a secret passage in the caves, probably with an exit either to the church or the Mausoleum. And is the 'mask of a witch' which Dashwood placed in a hole in the wall the clue to Churchill's picture of 'Fraud . . . in a dark corner, shunning sight of Man, and shrinking from the light'?

Let us turn from these baffling mysteries of the caves to the church and Mausoleum above, for the three are inextricably woven together and there are as many enigmas above ground as below it.

In Saxon England the village of Haveringdown stood on the top of West Wycombe Hill; it is said to have been a sizeable hamlet even before the Roman occupation of Britain. An ancient camp was situated where the Church of St. Lawrence now stands. The history of St. Lawrence's Church states: 'An old British camp . . . looking across to another camp at Desborough (*presumably Danesborough*) Castle, near the Church of SS. Mary and George, Sands (a large white building which can be seen on the right of the valley as you stand on the eastern side of the hill). In all probability the Britons built a church here and later their Saxon ancestors were converted to the faith by Saint Birinius, who preached the Gospel in the Thames Valley. The manor of West Wycombe is mentioned in Domesday Book and the first evidence of a church is found in the list of parish priests which begins in 1230. The church has outlived the village on the hill and has served as a parish church of West Wycombe.'

So here is yet another explanation of Wilkes's poser.

The church had fallen into disrepair nearly a century before Dashwood had it rebuilt. By 1639 it was stated to be 'in a sad and disreputable state'. After Sir Francis's renovation Mrs. Lybbe-Powys visited the church in 1775 and wrote this account of her impressions:

'It gives one not the least idea of a place sacred to religious worship. Tis a very superb Egyptian hall . . . the font is shown as an elegant toy: in fine, it has only the appearance of a neat ballroom with a row of forms on each side.'

Mrs. Lybbe-Powys's architectural knowledge must have been slight; there is nothing Egyptian about the church, but her unskilled eye must have misinterpreted the Corinthian pillars. It is difficult to reconcile these various views of the church as something unsuitable for religious worship with what one sees there today. The most remarkable feature of St. Lawrence's is the extraordinary blend of utilitarian puritanism with the bizarre. Whatever Francis planned, whatever little jokes he permitted himself in its construction, he never allowed his eccentricities in the renovation to go beyond the confines of good taste.

There is something Byzantine rather than pagan about the painted ceilings and plaster ornamentation of the interior of the church, something altogether foreign in the atmosphere of the place. But as the light changes, and the church is subject to the most astonishing metamorphoses as the sun's rays rise and fade, so one gets a series of vivid, kaleidoscopic effects which force a reappraisal of one's impressions. Langley must have had his feeling, for he wrote about the church's 'grimness' and 'terrifying aspect'

180

and then scratched out what he had set down. In one light the 'foreigness' dissolves; the bright light washes and purifies the whole scene and makes it wholesomely plain and English. Then, for a fleeting moment, the stone and marble paving of the centre aisle is reminiscent of St. Paul's Cathedral. Yet, at sunset, especially on a day that is brighter than usual, the feeling of an alien, sinister influence in the atmosphere returns and the interior of the church is suffused with a bizarre red limelight.

One biographer of Francis, Mr. Ronald Fuller, attributes this sense of the macabre to the superb painting of the Last Supper by Guiseppe Borgnis, which adorns the chancel ceiling. He draws attention to the eyes of Judas Iscariot which dominate the whole group and create an eerie effect. Certainly Judas attracts more attention than any other person in this beautifully executed work; he steals the picture by appearing so much more alive than any of the other figures, his eyes following one to every part of the chancel. Borgnis portrayed Judas in the act of suddenly turning round with a guilty and slightly malevolent stare. Perhaps the artist became fascinated by this character, though some have argued that he deliberately painted Judas like this on Dashwood's specific instructions. Another theory is that Borgnis's son, who completed the painting, added his own impression of Judas in touching up the original.

As to the Golden Ball, it must have required a steady nerve and a cool and sober head to climb up here, treading the narrow iron ladder, hand-railed with loose, swaying chains. At the top a trap door cut in the lower half of the globe is the only means of access. Inside the Ball are three narrow seats – cramped accommodation for any relaxation and the drinking of 'divine milk punch'.

Interesting is the sun-dial erected by Dashwood on the south side of the church, bearing the legend: 'Keep thy tongue from evil speaking, lying and slandering.' Doubtless even then he knew how many wild stories were being bandied about him and the Brotherhood.

Restoration work on the Mausoleum was begun in 1956, and busts of Bubb Dodington, Lady Austin and Rachel

Antonina have been reproduced. An empty pedestal now marks the site of a bust to 'Thomas Thompson, M.D.', mentioned by Langley. This refers to the friend of Dodington and Whitehead and former physician to the Prince of Wales.

The cenotaph to the memory of Sarah, Baroness le Despencer 'who finished a most exemplary life on January 19, 1769', bears this tribute:

'May this cenotaph be
Sacred to the Virtues and Graces
That constitute Female Excellence
Perpetually.'

The old village rhyme which has been quoted earlier in this chapter was given to the Dashwood family by an old lady who could only remember three lines, but who claimed that alogether there were six verses.

Mr. H. N. Melford, an authority on the legends of old English villages, made some research into the rhyme about the 'twenty steps' several years ago, but without arriving at any definite conclusions. As far as he could ascertain the rhyme 'originated round about 1780–1800, when it was often quoted in West Wycombe. What baffled him at first was why one should take a pick to find a stile, but he was convinced that the word 'stile' was used not to convey the idea of wooden steps over a fence, or a gate, but in its rarer meaning of a vertical piece in a panelled door. The word 'stile' was sometimes used in the sense of a secret panel.

Thus the 'twenty steps' could very well be the steps of the secret passage in the cave and the 'stile' a secret panel in a door long since blocked in by stones which could only be removed by a pick. This would make sense of another verse which Melford recalled:

''twas twenty-two in Dashwood's time,
Perhaps to hide this cell divine
Where lay my love in peace sublime.'

The riddle becomes even more puzzling. Is the 'twenty-two' a reference to the 'XXIIF' carved on the wall of the caves? Is the suggestion that Dashwood deliberately sought to mislead some person or persons who might be trying to locate a secret cell in the cave? And who was 'my love'? These questions might be answered if someone in Buckinghamshire could come forward with the missing verses.

Meanwhile there is one possible solution. I fear that like the research into Hall Stevenson's verse it destroys any romantic wishful thinking, the hope of revealing some dark scandal or Poesque love mystery that might lie behind the tangle of obscure poems and village jingles. Lord Le Despencer had a daughter by the mistress who looked after him in his declining years, the actress Frances Barry, former paramour of a Ludgate Hill mercer. In 1774 was born Rachel Antonina Lee, a strange, oddly beautiful child who grew into an even stranger and more attractive young woman.

Rachel Antonina had many of her father's qualities; indeed, she possessed all his quirks and eccentricities magnified a thousandfold, his passion for secrecy and mystery, his interest in the occult. But she lacked her father's redeeming common sense, his practical mind and self-discipline. Perhaps on so sensitive a mind the harsh fact of her illegitimacy preyed more deeply than others could possibly imagine. She later claimed that her father had secretly married her mother and that the marriage documents had been hidden by the Dashwood family. She insisted, wrongly, in calling herself Baroness le Despencer and railed against her father's sister[1] who also used the same title quite improperly. Sir Thomas Stapleton took the barony, while Sir John Dashwood-King, Francis's step-brother, became the next baronet. Rachel Antonina's *Remarks on a Will*, published in 1828, throw some light on the controversy which raged on these problems of succession.

But Antonina allowed her sense of fantasy to upset her judgments and the world at large regarded her as completely mad. Had she been born sooner, she might have made the perfect companion for her father. She was all her life the prototype of Oscar Wilde's heroine in his short story, *A*

1. Rachel, widow of Sir Robert Austin.

Sphinx Without A Secret, even to the point, or so it is suspected, of staging her own kidnapping.

Where her father had been a benevolent patron of the Church of England, and kept his agnosticism for his intimates, Antonina openly and brazenly boasted of her atheism, refusing in court to take the oath as a Christian and conveying such violent views to one rector that he said she 'breathed sentiments fresh from the mintage of hell'. Thomas de Quincey described her as 'a magnificent witch' and indeed her portraits suggest a wild-eyed, elfin Emma Hamilton.

One of her peculiarities was to write coded messages on scraps of paper and leave them in various hiding places; these messages when decoded were full of Brontesque fantasy and told of the make-believe world in which Rachel Antonina lived. She revelled in secret passages and caves and perhaps as a child she was taken to see those at West Wycombe by her father. She told various people that 'the clue to all my troubles can be found in the heart of the hill.'[1]

It might be that the legend of the secret passage was fostered and elaborated by Rachel Antonina and that she was the authoress of the village jingle. Certainly it would be in keeping with her love of a romantic dream world of exotic mystery, conjured up out of her own riotous and abandoned imagination.

After her death a collection of books on the occult were found among her possessions, but there was no trace of the private papers her father was supposed to have left her. Many pages from the books were missing, whether torn out by her or her father one cannot tell. There was a manuscript of *Kama Sutra*, obviously laboriously copied from a rough translation of the original and bearing the inscription from 'Henry Vansittart to the Founder'. This seems to confirm that Henry Vansittart did pass on this ancient sexual handbook for the instruction of the Franciscans.

1. De Quincey.

CHAPTER 11

TWILIGHT YEARS OF THE FRANCISCANS

IT has been often stated that the last meeting of the Franciscans took place at Medmenham in June 1762. But there is conclusive evidence that, though this may have been the last Chapter before political dissensions rent the society in twain, Medmenham Abbey was still being used by the club as late as 1770.

Within a few years the society was not only depleted by resignations and possibly expulsions, but by death. The Duffields, Potter, Dodington, Churchill and Lloyd had all died and some of the aristocrats who had begged so eagerly to be allowed to join in the early 'sixties now shied away from the Medmenhamites as though the latter were contaminated. Gossip, malicious pamphlets and the charges against Wilkes had done their damage.

As a result whatever activities were continued at the Abbey must have been drastically curtailed, for the site was allowed to fall into disrepair. Surreptitious visits were paid by such inveterate gossipmongers as Horace Walpole, who prowled around the Abbey making notes. To some extent Medmenham may have been deliberately maintained as the formal headquarters for the club in order to cover up the new meeting place in the caves. And, as we have already seen, the secret of the caves was well guarded.

In July 1768 there appeared in the *Political Register* a letter which asked: 'Is there or was there not some time ago subsisting in the county of Kent a society of gentlemen bearing the name of the Franciscan Friars?'

Thus it will be seen that within five years the activities of the Franciscans had largely been forgotten by the public, so much so that the county of their adoption had been mistaken for Kent.

Yet it is just possible that this was a subtle inquiry by someone who suspected that the headquarters might have been moved to Kent. For Lord le Despencer had in this period paid frequent visits to Mereworth in Kent, where his uncle, the Earl of Westmorland, had been carrying out extensive work on his Italianate castle. Le Despencer's influence can be seen today in Mereworth Church, the oddest in the county, with its six great columns supporting a portico, a tower rising like a needle in the sky, and thirty-six sham marble columns down the narrow aisles.

A letter from Benjamin Franklin to a Mr. Acourt, of Philadelphia, mentioned 'the exquisite sense of classical design, charmingly reproduced by the Lord le Despencer at West Wycombe, whimsical and puzzling as it may sometimes be in its imagery, is as evident below the earth as above it.' This must surely be a reference to the caves, and one can only assume that some of the statuary from Medmenham's gardens found a resting place in the subterranean headquarters of the Franciscans.

There is a curious story told about a visit paid by Franklin to West Wycombe in 1772. Accompanied by Dashwood and others, Franklin paid a visit to grottoes near by. The talk touched upon the subject of miracles and the occult. Amused at such unscientific chatter, Franklin, who, according to Paul Whitehead, was a great practical joker, offered to perform for the company the miracle of bringing peace to stormy waters. Incredulous, they challenged him to make good his boast.

Franklin then led the way up some steps to a crevice where he could look down on a subterranean stream whose waters were agitated like a cauldron. While the others remained at the water's edge, holding torches, Franklin waved his stick in the manner of a magician and pronounced some mumbo-jumbo. The onlookers below were astonished to notice that the water became strangely still.

Laughingly, Franklin descended and asked the company what they thought of his 'miracle'. Then he explained that in the end of his cane he had secreted some oil and that all he had done was to allow some drops of this to trickle down to the stream.

Was this subterranean stream the 'Styx'? Van Doren

gives the details of this story in his biography of Franklin, but his version suggests that the incident occurred at some lake in the vicinity of West Wycombe House.

It is also claimed that Franklin was a visitor to Borgnis's cave at Marlow – apparently he was a keen speleologist – and on a visit to an inn at Marlow the landlord once asked: 'Is not that Master Franklin?' 'No,' he was told, 'it is Brother Benjamin of Cookham.' There was much mirth at this reply.

In the wine books of the society there are references to 'Brother Francis of Cookham' and 'Brother Thomas of Cookham', but none to 'Brother Benjamin'. It would almost seem that 'Brothers of Cookham' was used as an alias in certain circumstances – another puzzling conundrum.

The next published reference to the society was a statement in *Town and Country* in 1773, which told how it had 'phoenix-like arisen from out of its flames', with the suggestion that the Franciscans had taken on 'a new lease of their mysterious lives in some hiding place in the country-side.'

The Franciscans may have had several 'homes' at this period. Yet the wine books show that the society was functioning at Medmenham in 1769 and in 1774. There is even an inventory of kitchen utensils, glass, furniture, and 'forty prints of heads of Kings with black frames and glazed; ninety small prints of Monks etc.', dated 1774. One must assume that the *et cetera* included portraits of the 'Nuns.'

Three years later the *Morning Post* of 22 August, 1776, carried this notice: 'The Order of the Franciscan Society at Medmenham being nearly demolished, J——y Twitcher,[1] who is almost the only surviving member of that club (formerly called the Hell-Fire Club), is determined to restore it to its original glory; in consequence of which intention we hear he has taken down the Circumnavigator and W. Salamander in order to initiate them into that infernal society.'

1. Lord Sandwich's nickname.

The 'Circumnavigator' was Sir Joseph Banks (1744–1820) President of the Royal Society, known by his nickname on account of his navigational exploits. In 1766 he made a voyage to Newfoundland, where he collected plants; later, at his own expense, he fitted out a vessel in which he accompanied Captain Cook on his voyage round the world. He was a great authority on Tahiti, which might explain Sandwich's interest in him, as the former First Lord had always been eager to have first-hand information from voyagers in the Pacific.

'W. Salamander,' however, may not have been a real person, but a piece of satirical make-believe. The writer of this item of gossip was possibly trying to picture the erudite Banks introducing to the society the poison-ejecting salamander.[1]

The last remaining members of the Franciscans probably did not number more than half a dozen, possibly le Despencer, Sandwich, Sir Thomas Stapleton, Dr. Benjamin Bates, Henry Vansittart and Sir John Dashwood-King, who, according to Lipscomb, was the last surviving member of the society. By the late 'seventies they must have been wearying of the worship of Venus, if still invoking Bacchus. The introduction of such eminent men of science as Franklin and Banks must to some extent have transformed their activities.

Meanwhile le Despencer was still busily devoting himself to the renovation of West Wycombe House and the replanning of the park. The classical house, situated on the southern slope of a wooded valley, with the River Wye flowing in the distance, and the cone-shaped hill of West Wycombe in the background, provided a superb environment for imaginative garden-making. Until 1740 the gardens had been formal and terraced, but le Despencer, with the aid of 'Capability' Brown and his pupil, Thomas Cook, altered all that.

In the manuscript notes of Langley's *Hundred of Desborough* there appears a pencilled marginal comment on some of the latter-day activities of le Despencer, showing

[1]. It could have been Joseph Salvador, F.R.S.

that he never lost his love of masquerade even in his old age. In fact, he seemed anxious that not only the Medmenhamites, but the public, too, should share in the fun of pagan pageantry and imbibe something of the spirit of classical masques. For Langley records that in September, 1771:

'The delightful gardens at the seat of Lord le Despencer at West Wycombe were opened to the public and a novel exhibition took place in one of the rural walks. A fine portico at the west end of the house has been lately erected (in imitation of that of the Temple of Bacchus) for the dedication of which a Bacchanalian procession was formed of Bacchanals, Priests, Priestesses, Pan, Fauns, Satyrs, Silenus, etc., all in proper habits and skins wreathed with vine leaves, ivy, oak, etc.

'On the arrival of the procession in the portico the High Priest addressed the Statue in an Invocation which was succeeded by several hymns, and other pieces of music vocal and instrumental suitable to the occasion, and having finished the sacrifice proceeded through the groves to a Tent pitched among several others at the head of the lake where the Paeans and libations were repeated – then ferrying to a vessel adorned with colours and streamers, again performed various ceremonies with discharges of cannon and bursts of acclamations from the populace.

'The ceremony was finished by a congratulatory address or ode to the Deity of the place. Several of the company wore masques on this occasion.'

Here again is proof of the comparative harmlessness of the Franciscans. Had this masquerade been performed in the caves at West Wycombe it would undoubtedly have been dubbed a 'satanic orgy'. Produced in the park for the benefit of the public, it sounds as innocent as a church pageant.

In his statuary in the park and in the paintings he commissioned for West Wycombe House, Lord le Despencer delighted in recording classical myth and pagan frolics. The colourful ceiling of the dining-room illustrates the story of Cupid and Psyche and the admission of Psyche to the 'celestial hierarchy', while in the blue drawing-room the ceiling panel is a copy of Annibale Caracci's 'Triumph of Bacchus and Ariadne', with the attendant procession of fauns and satyrs of which he never seemed to tire.

Nor did he seem to find anything incongruous in interlarding pictures of Biblical scenes with classical paintings of a frankly pagan and hedonistic character. Another point worth noting is that le Despencer was not an artistic snob, nor did he buy or commission paintings for their intrinsic value. Though he acquired a collection of pictures by Hogarth, Romney and Zoffany, he did not show them at West Wycombe House. This he reserved almost exclusively for copies of the work of illustrious Italians and for original works of lesser artists. His main aim seemed to be to satisfy his personal whims and to decorate the walls and ceilings with interpretations of his favourite themes. One notes that his choice of Biblical subjects was also not without significance – 'The Creation of Eve', 'The Fall' and 'Abraham Entertaining the Three Angels'.

Only occasionally in these later years were there further published references to the society. A book called *The Fruit Shop* hinted that the club had been formed for 'political reasons'. But, though it foundered through Parliamentary squabbles, there is no truth in this assertion. An Italian writer, Amalfi, mentioned that Prince Charles Edward Stuart on his march into England had 'planned to meet Sir Charles Dashwood on his way to London' and told how 'the Order of Sir Francis', a pro-Jacobite organization in Buckinghamshire, was 'in readiness to receive and assist His Royal Highness'. There is not a word of truth in this assertion, for the society was not formed in 1745, but it is typical of the wild rumours which the 'Jacobite scare' produced not only in England but on the Continent. Mlle Perrault writes: 'There is no evidence that I know of that in any way links the Franciscans with the adherents of the Young Pretender. In fact, quite the reverse. The Chevalier D'Eon was asked by the French Government to inquire into the "political purposes" of the Franciscans and (according to Lèon

Perrault) he had to report that there was nothing in the society to warrant investigation and that the reports of Jacobitism were utterly unfounded.'

In a faded bunch of newspaper clippings of the eighteenth century discovered a few years before World War II this curious notice appears under a column headed 'Miscellaneous Intelligence': 'At the Fair at Tenterden this week passed by a most remarkable exhibit of somewhat awe-inspiring and horrific appearance was shewn to the assembled populace. The said exhibit consisting as it did of the skeleton of a human hand bearing rings thereon shocked the susceptibilities of all present. This most grewsome (*sic*) article, contained in a glass case, was stated to have been conveyed from the Dog and Badger alehouse at a place called Meadham on the River Thames, where, it may be recollected, that some years ago there was in existence a society most foul and bestial in its nefarious deeds, appropriately named the Hell-Fire Club. The exhibit is believed to be a relic of this society's satanic practices.'

The date of this cutting was 1779. Unfortunately there was nothing to indicate what journal produced this strange piece of provincial 'intelligence'; it was almost certainly a provincial paper, probably a Kentish weekly published in Tenterden, which in those days boasted of both its own newspaper and theatre, neither of which it possesses today.

This is more than another example of how credulous people accepted the most ridiculous stories about the Franciscans, for one must suppose that 'Meadham' referred to Medmenham. I am indebted to Mr. C. J. Pytchley for this addition to the story:

'I was led to examine the account of the skeleton hand through my hobby of collecting data on ghost stories. What struck me forcibly about this story was that I was sure I had heard something very like it before.

'Then I recollected that in *Lord Halifax's Ghost Book*, Volume II, there is a tale entitled "The Bloody Hand", which tells of a skeleton human hand carrying two rings, which was put in a glass case in a public house.

'I was not able to discover whether there was any link between this tale told by Lord Halifax and the skeleton hand exhibited at Tenterden, but I did learn there was a vague legend about a "Bloody Hand" which had been village gossip down at Marlow, near Medmenham, about 200 years ago. Apparently the skeleton hand of a female was found in some woods and I am told it was used for a gruesome gambling game at the Dog and Badger Inn. As far as I can gather to each throw of a dice, the index finger was moved so many places.

'If at the end of the game, it pointed straight at one of the players, he had to wear the hand, strapped on his wrist, until his gambling debts were settled – sometimes several weeks later.'

There is no confirmation of this story in Marlow or Medmenham, but it has parallels in two separate ghost stories told by a Mr. Piercey, who was a member of West Wycombe Parish Council for many years. Mr. Piercey has mentioned the ghost of 'the Spangled Lady of Sandage Wood, a discarded victim of the Hell-Fire Club', who found a 'watery grave in the bogs of Widdington Park'. He also refers to yet another ghost – 'Old Bloody Bones' of Castlefield not far from West Wycombe.

There is, however, no positive evidence of any female Medmenhamite having been found drowned, but it seems likely that this story is the sole basis of the fantasy that the Franciscans kidnapped local wenches and removed them to the caves! The 'Spangled Lady' may have been a member of a gypsy tribe that lived in the neighbourhood, as West Wycombe and Seer both had colonies of gypies two hundred years ago.

Mr. Ronald Fuller in *Hell-Fire Francis* told how a stain 'like five red fingers appeared on the marble of a mural tablet in the chancel' of St. Lawrence's Church to the memory of the first Sir Francis. It would seem from this account that this strange manifestation occurred during the last few years of Lord le Despencer's life. The 'superstitious villagers', he added, referred to it as 'The Bloody Hand'. All attempts to wash it off failed.

A visit to this church today will provide proof of a reddish stain on the mural, though it would require a lively imagination to decipher it as five red finger-prints. No one locally seems to have heard of the legend mentioned by Mr. Fuller, not even present members of the Dashwood family. Nor can anyone suggest how the stain came there.

When Johnston's revised version of *Chrysal*, containing the alleged description of the Medmenham orgies, was published, it was soon in great demand, and, as a result, crowds of people flocked down to see the Abbey and even broke down fences to go souvenir-hunting in the gardens. Perhaps these activities induced the Duffield family to part with the Medmenham estates; at any rate the Abbey was sold by them to John Morton, Chief Justice of Chester, in 1779.

Thus in his declining years Lord le Despencer saw the last links between his society and Medmenham severed and one by one the remaining members died. His closest friend in these last days was Dr. Bates, who conscientiously nursed him through a long illness so that he began to recover something of his old sparkle and express a desire to revisit his beloved Italy. He took the keenest interest in planning this trip: all arrangements were made and Dr. Bates was to accompany him. Then, quite suddenly, on the eve of their departure, he was taken ill again. On 11 December, 1781, the founder of the Franciscans passed peacefully away. He was laid to rest in the family vault at St. Lawrence's Church, where a grey marble tablet, erected by his sister Rachel, records that he was 'revered, beloved and regretted by all who knew him'.

With his death the last vestiges of the society disappeared for ever. 'Saint' Francis himself had always been almost the sole *raison d'être* for the club and there was no other member left with either the youth, imagination, vigour or personality to revive it. Unlike Dodington and Whitehead, Francis made no melodramatic gesture in his will, nor did he leave instructions for any memorial to the club and its members. The joke had been played out; Venus and Bacchus must have seemed faint wraiths of their former selves. Dr. Bates lived on until into his nineties, but he resolutely refused to commit his memories of the society to paper, contenting himself with indignant repudiations of the wild stories that continued to circulate about the episodes at Medmenham. Sir John Dashwood-King also maintained silence about the club.

In 1786 the Abbey was sold by John Morton's widow to one Robert Scott. Later the building was converted into an inn and various attempts were made to capitalize the legends of the Franciscans. Trippers were encouraged to come up the Thames to the Ferry Boat Inn and the Dog and Badger to view the 'Haunts of the Rake-Hells of Medmenham'. Boatmen earned handsome tips for showing them the 'cradles' in which the 'Monks' were supposed to have slept. It might be added that the 'cradles' were put there by the exploiters of the Abbey. In 1803 a Miss Beamish wrote an account of a visit to the Abbey: 'Not even the new school of so-called romantic thought could pierce the gloom of Medmenham and find a single joyful motif in this sombre scene. All is decay. This surprises me not in the least when I consider the ridiculous fabrications of some vulgar persons who have endeavoured to invent what they failed to find. To talk of cradles at Medmenham is a preposterous suggestion. The only cradle ever known there belonged to the caretaker, a Mistress Edgerley.'

So, once again, Sophia Edgerley's name appears. It seems likely that this was the old servant to whom Langley spoke.

By the beginning of the nineteenth century the chapel of the Abbey had completely disappeared and slowly interest in Medmenham evaporated. But imitators of the society occasionally popped up unexpectedly and tried to recapture the mad merriment of those bygone days. One learns that 'on one of the little islands of the Thames near Marlow Barrymore conducted midnight orgies'. Byron was also guilty of perpetuating the 'Hell-Fire' legend. He insisted that the Franciscans were 'worshippers of Satan', and in

1809 held a meeting of fellow roisterers at Newstead Abbey where, in memory of Medmenham, they drank burgundy from a human skull and dressed up as 'emissaries from Hades'. Byron was the originator of the falsehood that the Franciscans drank their wine from human skulls.

As the middle of the nineteenth century approached Victorianism raised its censorial head. No longer did the curious come to stare at Medmenham. Instead irate Puritans and fanatical crack-pot Dissenters set out to pillage and destroy all traces of the society at West Wycombe. How thoroughly they succeeded we do not know, but the local newspapers of the period recorded such incidents as the theft of Paul Whitehead's heart from the Mausoleum, acts of vandalism to memorials and inscriptions in this temple to Dodington's memory and various attacks on the Church of St. Lawrence. In the Mausoleum busts were knocked down and tablets chipped and defaced, while in 1845 someone piled prayer books round the font of the church and tried to burn it to the ground.

The revolt against rakemanship was under way, and with it came the unspoken, but implicit demand that the aristocracy should be put in a strait-jacket which would make originality a vice and mediocrity a virtue. That some change in the structure of society was needed for political and ethical reasons, few would deny, but that the metamorphosis engendered by the industrial revolution should anaesthetize the aristocracy into a uniform dullness was deplorable. An empire can be – indeed, usually is – built by rake-hells and eccentrics; it cannot be sustained by a strait-jacket leadership imposed by unimaginative militarism on the one hand and the inhibitions of Dr. Arnold on the other.

One must not allow sentimental prejudices to be dressed up in the respectable clothes of a would-be interpreter of history. To assert that the British Empire was inspired and created through the influence of such men as the rakes of Medmenham is as outrageous as to dub them as satanists and decadents. But, capricious, wayward, wanton and madcap as the Medmenhamites may have been, they are something more than an excuse for a nostalgic yearning for more spacious days. There are certain facts about the decline and fall of rakemanship which explain in part at least the political and social sins of omission which have besotted British life for more than a century.

Rhetorical and flamboyant as it may sound, the catalogue of these facts is not unimpressive. When the rake disappeared, much that was great, intellectually, politically and even spiritually went with him. The Grand Tour was frowned upon; education was so illiberal and insular that it became the habit for Foreign Secretaries to boast that they never travelled abroad. The 'Nelson touch', symbol of naval rakemanship, gave place to the crass stupidities of 'Theirs not to reason why.' The rake with his masquerades was supplanted by the stay-at-home Victorian squire and his platitudes; Italianate follies and Palladian loveliness were submerged by hideous architectural excrescences which stuck like scabs to the masterpieces of the past. The Georgian Age may not have been a golden age, but it was the one age when in England the artist, the writer and the poet were honoured, when intellectualism and art flowered even in rake-hell clubs. If the novel of France was born in the cafés of Paris, then modern English literature was nursed in such institutions as the Dilettanti, the Divan and to some extent the Order of 'Saint' Francis. Even more important, these social and artistic developments were not hot-house flowers gathered by feverish cliques, but sturdy plants, watered by Tory and Whig alike, by middle-class poets and painters as well as by aristocratic Roaring Boys and exhibitionists.

When rakemanship mellowed into clubmanship as great a service was done to the English heritage as anything achieved by the Wesleyans, the Tolpuddle Martyrs or the capitalist-humbugs of the Manchester School of Liberals. This alliance of the rake and the clubman, of rich aristocrat and impoverished artist produced Pope, Dr. Johnson, Charles Churchill, Hogarth, Sterne, Clive, Vansittart, Wilkes, Joshua Reynolds, Quin, Foote, Bannister, Colman, Goldsmith, Fielding and Smollett. It gave us Banks as well as Sandwich. Nash as well as Dashwood. It raised not only follies and grottoes, but a new and noble London in the place of what had been little more than a Cockney Copenhagen. True, it did not save England from the exacerbations of Lord North's policy and the blunder over the American colonies. But Lord North was neither a clubman, nor a rake; he was so insular, so lacking in the conversational talents which the clubmen had that, we are told, he was 'speechless in the presence of Benjamin Franklin'. Yet Franklin was the friend of the Franciscans, while the men who held the English standard in North America were not honest-to-goodness British rakes, but dull, unthinking Hessian levies.

One does not today put up a memorial to the magistrates who deported the Tolpuddle Martyrs. But nor ought one to perpetuate the latter-day picture of Georgian England as a cesspool where the wicked, demented rakes crushed down the poor, half-starved heroic working classes.

The Franciscans, in their own peculiar way, represented a balance between these two extreme viewpoints. But the pendulum of their hectic career never swung too wildly one way or the other. Amid all their follies and pranks a certain element of radical humanism peeps out – the humanism of Rabelais and Sterne. Play-acting did not beget humbug; it helped to dispel it. Indeed there is no better example of their ability to laugh at themselves and to eschew pretence than these lines of Robert Lloyd's:

> 'You know, dear George, I'm none of those
> That condescend to write in prose:
> Inspir'd with pathos and sublime,
> I always soar – in doggrel rhyme:
> And scarce can ask you how you do,
> Without a jingling line or two.
> Besides, I always took delight in
> What bears the name of easy writing;
> Perhaps the reason makes it please
> Is that I find 'tis writ with ease.'

LIST OF PERSONS BELIEVED TO BE MEMBERS OF THE ORDER OF
'SAINT' FRANCIS OF WYCOMBE

Members of the 'Inner Circle'

SIR FRANCIS DASHWOOD, BARON LE DESPENCER. Chancellor
of the Exchequer and Postmaster-General.

PAUL WHITEHEAD. Poet, pamphleteer and High Steward of
the Society.

JOHN MONTAGU, EARL OF SANDWICH. First Lord of the
Admiralty.

GEORGE BUBB DODINGTON (LORD MELCOMBE REGIS).
Member of Parliament.

THOMAS POTTER, Paymaster-General, Treasurer for Ireland
and son of the Archbishop of Canterbury.

SIR THOMAS STAPLETON. Cousin of Sir Francis Dashwood.

SIR WILLIAM STANHOPE, Son of Lord Chesterfield.

SIR JOHN DASHWOOD-KING. Half-brother to Sir Francis
Dashwood and Member of Parliament.

FRANCIS DUFFIELD. Soldier, artist and landowner at Medmenham.

ROBERT VANSITTART. Scholar and Member of Parliament.

MR. CLARKE of Henley.

Members Whose Claims Have Been
Established by Several Sources

JOHN WILKES. Member of Parliament and Lord Mayor of
London.

CHARLES CHURCHILL. Poet and clergyman.

ROBERT LLOYD. Poet and dramatist.

GEORGE SELWYN. Member of Parliament and Wit.

DR. BENJAMIN BATES. Scholar of Aylesbury.

SIR JOHN D'AUBREY. Magistrate.

GIUSEPPE BORGNIS. Italian painter.

JAMES DUFFIELD. Rake.

ARTHUR VANSITTART. Member of Parliament.
HENRY VANSITTART. Governor of Bengal.
WILLIAM HOGARTH, Painter.
RICHARD HOPKINS. Wealthy landowner.
HENRY LOVIBOND COLLINS. Poet.
GEORGE, THIRD EARL OF ORFORD.
SIR FRANCIS DELAVAL.

Probable Members

FREDERICK, PRINCE OF WALES.
THE EARL OF BUTE. Prime Minister.
DR. THOMAS THOMPSON. One-time physician to Frederick, Prince of Wales.
SIMON LUTTRELL.
JOHN FANE, SEVENTH EARL OF WESTMORLAND.
HENRY FOX (LORD HOLLAND).
EVELYN PIERREPONT, DUKE OF KINGSTON.
JOHN MANNERS, MARQUIS OF GRANBY.
JOHN HALL STEVENSON. Poet and satirist.
WILLIAM DOUGLAS, EARL OF MARCH. Rake.
NICHOLAS REVETT. Architect.

Possible and Doubtful Members

BENJAMIN FRANKLIN. Statesman and philosopher.
HORACE WALPOLE. Politician and author.
EDMUND DUFFIELD. Vicar of Medmenham.
TIMOTHY SHAW. Vicar of Medmenham.
HENRY EDMUND STEVENS. Landowner at Medmenham.
HENRY VANHATTAN.
CHEVALIER D'EON DE BEAUMONT. French diplomat.
GIOVANNI BORGNIS. Son of the painter.
JOHN DUFFIELD.
LAWRENCE STERNE. Novelist and satirist.
SIR JOSEPH BANKS. President of the Royal Society, explorer and botanist.
THE HONOURABLE JACK SPENCER. Rake.
W. SALAMANDER. Included as a very 'doubtful' member on

the evidence of the *Morning Post*. This may refer to JOSEPH SALVADOR, another member of the Royal Society and a friend of DASHWOOD.

LORD GEORGE CAVENDISH.

LORD GEORGE LYTTLETON. His bust was included among the collection of models of society members.

COUNT ALBINI. Of Udine in Tivoli, in the Venetian State.

DR. JAMES MOUNSEY. Physician to the Army of Russia.

It is impossible to prepare any accurate list of the female members of the society, but there are some grounds, slender enough, for mentioning the following as possible members:

FANNY MURRAY. Courtesan of Bath and London. One-time mistress of Beau Nash and the Earl of Sandwich and wife of David Ross the actor.

AGNES (or MARY) PERRAULT. One-time bookseller's assistant and wife of a French merchant.

CHARLOTTE HAYES. London bordello-keeper and probably an agent for the society.

ELIZABETH ROACH. Believed to have been a mistress of Sir Francis Dashwood.

LUCY COOPER. Also reputed to have been Dashwood's mistress.

SOPHIA EDGERLEY. Wife of an inhabitant of Medmenham and said to have held a 'situation' at the Abbey.

FRANCIS, VISCOUNTESS VANE. Authoress of *The Memoirs of a Lady of Quality*.

BETTY WEYMS. A courtesan noted for her glass eye, which she was always losing at the Rose Tavern.

MARY WALCOT. Half-sister of Sir Francis Dashwood.

LADY MARY WORTLEY-MONTAGU. Her membership is very dubious, though she would appear to have been a member of the Divan Club and was certainly an old friend of Dashwood.

LADY BETTY GERMAIN.

CHEVALIER D'EON DE BEAUMONT. (Also mentioned as one of the male members.) No reference has been made in the book to his having been one of the 'Nuns' owing to his membership in any capacity being extremely doubtful. But malicious gossip, based on the controversy on his sex and his masquerades in female attire, alleged that he 'played the part of a Mollie at Medmenham'. The author, while rejecting this theory, believes it should be mentioned.

The Hundred of Desborough. Thomas Langley, 1797.

Chrysal: The Adventures of a Guinea. Charles Johnston. 1760 and 1821.

Benjamin Franklin. Carl Van Doren. 1939.

Nocturnal Revels. Anonymous. 1779.

Life and Poems of Paul Whitehead. Edward Thompson. 1777.

New Foundling Hospital for Wits. John Almon and John Wilkes.

Clubs of the Georgian Rakes. Louis C. Jones. 1942.

Correspondence of John Wilkes and Charles Churchill. E. H. Weatherley. 1954.

Hell-Fire Club: King's Order in Council. 1721.

Satan's Harvest Home. Anonymous. 1749.

Liturgies. Francis Dashwood (Baron le Despencer) and Benjamin Franklin, 1773.

Remarks on a Will. Rachel F. A. Lee. 1828.

Bulletin of the John Rylands Library, Manchester, Volume xxxvii, No. 1 (Containing some letters of Sir Francis Dashwood). 1954.

Patron and Place Hunter. Charles Lloyd Sanders. (A biography of Bubb Dodington.) 1919.

Charles Churchill. Wallace C. Brown. 1953.

Hell-Fire Francis. Ronald Fuller. 1939.

Diary of George Bubb. 1784.

Curious Letters. Benjamin Franklin. 1898.

The Manor and Parish of Medmenham. The Rev. Arthur Plaisted. 1925.

Lives of the Rakes. Volume iv. Edwin Beresford Chancellor.

London Magazine. December 1763.

Journal of Ex-Libris Society. April 1901.

Sir Richard Escombe. Sir Max Pemberton. 1910.

History of Buckinghamshire. George Lipscomb. 1847.

Correspondence of John Wilkes. John Almon. 1805.

That Devil Wilkes. Raymond Postgate. 1930.

The Works of John Hall Stevenson. 1795.

Crazy Tales. John Hall Stevenson. 1772.

Ladies Fair and Frail. Bleackley. 1909.

The Temple of Venus. Edward Thompson. 1763.

Journals of Visits to Country Seats. Horace Walpole. 1928.

The Egerton MSS. The British Museum.

Worthies of Buckinghamshire. R. Gibbs.

The Theory and Practice of Landscape Gardening. Humphrey Repton. 1803.

The Public Advertiser. 1763.

The Life, Adventures, Intrigues and Amours of the Celebrated Jemmy Twitcher. J. Brough. 1770.

The Political Register. 1768.

Town and Country. 1773.

Morning Post. 1776.

Follies and Grottoes. Barbara Jones.

Beauties of Stowe. George Bickham. 1753.

The Diaries of Mrs. Phillip Lybbe-Powys.

Historical Memoirs of My Own Time. Sir Nathaniel Wraxall. 1815.

Memoirs of the Reign of King George III. Horace Walpole (edited by Marchant, 1845).

The North Briton, 1762.

Black Magic titles by Dennis Wheatley
published by Arrow Books

THE DEVIL RIDES OUT

GATEWAY TO HELL

THE HAUNTING OF TOBY JUGG

THE KA OF GIFFORD HILLARY

THE SATANIST

STRANGE CONFLICT

THEY USED DARK FORCES

TO THE DEVIL – A DAUGHTER

A serious study of the Occult, fully illustrated
THE DEVIL AND ALL HIS WORKS

If you would like a complete list of Arrow Books, including
other Dennis Wheatley titles, please send a postcard to:
P.O. Box 29, Douglas, Isle of Man, Great Britain.